DR WILLIAM PRICE
– SAINT OR SINNER?

Dr William Price
SAINT OR SINNER?

Cyril Bracegirdle

ISBN: 0-86381-434-4

Cover design: Alan Jones

First published in 1997 by Gwasg Carreg Gwalch,
12 Iard yr Orsaf, Llanrwst, Wales LL26 0EH
☎ (01492) 642031
Printed and published in Wales.

Dr William Price in druid costume
(Photo: courtesy of Welsh Folk Museum)

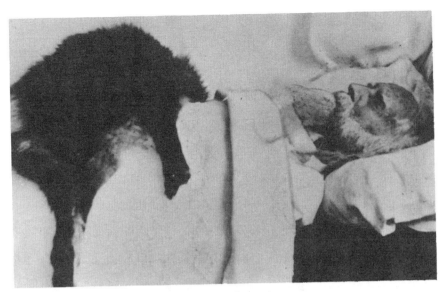

Dr William Price lying in state.

Cremation of Dr William Price, 1893.

A postcard in memoriam of Dr Price

Contents

Chapter 1

The Chartist

Lightning did not flash nor thunder roll on March 4, 1800, when a third son was born to the Rev. William Price and his wife Mary, but it should have done, for this was the start of a stormy career that was to span all but the last seven years of the 19th century.

In the little rural Welsh community of Rudry, in what is now mid-Glamorgan, it was customary for the birth to be marked by the gathering of the nearest relatives to offer thanksgiving to God for the arrival of another soul on earth, and this was done in the parlour of their small cottage.

We may wonder what those simple, God-fearing folk would have thought if there had been an astrologer on hand to say, 'This boy will become an atheist and will reject all your beliefs. He will pioneer the practice of burning the bodies of the deceased instead of normal Christian burial. He will become a famous man of medicine but will be persecuted by other medical men. He will be a leader of a revolutionary movement as yet unborn. He will be visited by strange fantasies and will be denounced from every pulpit in the land. Most shocking of all – he will live with women out of wedlock.'

But there were no omens to warn them.

The boy, whom they baptised William after his father, grew up with three brothers and three sisters in a household which, though sometimes short of money, was never, so far as we know, actually poor. Such records as are available give no clue as to which church received the ministrations of the Rev. Price who was Church of England, not Welsh chapel.

In the little church at Bedwas there is a plaque on the north wall commemorating the Price family, which indicates that the Reverend was a person of some standing.

Only Welsh was spoken in the Price home, and William was sent to the school at Machen at the age of ten to learn English and a few other subjects. This was long before the Elementary Education Act of 1887 and there was no legal compulsion for a child to go to school. That William was sent was partly as an example of the family status and the fact that he very soon had shown an aptitude for study and a desire to learn.

After leaving school at 13 there seems to have been some indecision about his future, and for several months he loafed about at home, doing nothing, apparently – except to cause a lot of local comment. He spent much time walking in the hills reciting poetry aloud; unusual, perhaps, though probably less so in Wales than in England. However, his habit of stripping naked and lying on hillsides in the sun – and sometimes in the rain – was another matter. Even in the permissive 1990s such behaviour would hardly go unremarked!

'I hear the wind whispering in the trees,' he explained, when remonstrated with. 'I get energy from the sun, and the rain is pure.'

It was not an explanation that suited the conventions of the time. Asked what he wanted to do with his future, William replied that it was his ambition to be a doctor.

'A doctor, indeed,' said Price senior, shaking his head at such an unrealistic notion. 'There is no money in doctoring, boy. You would be better serving the church.'

'I have not seen a lot of money in the church,' William countered. 'Besides, it is people's bodies that I want to serve. I will leave souls – if they exist – to the priests.'

The Reverend gave way and sent him to be apprenticed to a Dr Evan Edwards at Caerphilly for five years. His duties were to study the pharmacopoeia, to mix medicines to the doctor's instructions, and to master the Latin dictionary.

Sometime during those five years the father seems to have died, and an Uncle Thomas appointed himself as the youngster's guardian. In 1820 Uncle Thomas decided that being an unpaid assistant to a mere doctor was no future for the son of a clergyman.

'I will have you appointed as assistant master at a school owned by a friend of mine. You will receive twenty pounds per annum, which is more than you would be likely to earn as a curate.'

The young Price stated bluntly that he did not intend to be either curate or assistant master. He would be a doctor. In that same year he went to London and enrolled at the Royal College of Surgeons. There is much in those early years of William Price that is obscure, and how or whence came the money to pay for him at the College is not known.

He astonished everyone by passing the examination of both College and Hall in 12 months, a feat that no student had succeeded in doing before. He spent another year studying anatomy, surgery, physiology and medicine. Having qualified in 1821 he returned to Wales and established a practice in the village of Nantgarw.

He was a big young man and made a striking figure, having let his hair grow in long plaits, and by this time he had taken to wearing a white tunic over a scarlet waistcoat with green trousers.

So eloquent was he that, confronted by his quick wit, ready tongue and scalpel-sharp mind, anyone of whom he required a service would usually end by doing what he wanted, awed into compliance. Sometimes he showed a strange, inflamed, flurried recklessness of action.

Eight miles from Cardiff, the Nantgarw area was short of doctors. However, as Price senior had commented, there was not a lot of money in doctoring. Price was generous to patients who were poor, and he seems to have used some good psychology in dealing with them.

While deploring the fact that people who were ill had to pay him for treatment, he nevertheless charged high fees to those whom he judged could afford, and his ability to cure began to earn him a reputation medically, while his comments on the methods of other doctors and on religion aroused much ire.

He expressed the opinion that doctors should be paid a regular fee for keeping their patients healthy. When people became ill then the doctor should bear the expense of treating them. He would probably have regarded our modern National Health Service as more of a national disease service.

He once gave a public lecture in which he said that 'Medical science has of all the sciences been the most unscientific (Bernard Shaw was to express the same opinion a hundred years later). Its professors, with a few exceptions such as myself, have always sought to cure disease by the magic of pills and potions and poisons that attack the ailment with the idea of suppressing the symptoms instead of attacking the cause.'

Price had become a vegetarian from his student days, and often put his patients on a natural food diet which, in a land dedicated to good Welsh lamb, was a heresy in itself.

It was while at Nantgarw that he became interested in Hindu literature and creeds and acquired, according to his own typically extravagant boast, a knowledge of the majority of Western languages and a few of the Eastern ones. Certainly he does seem to have been a fluent linguist.

At this period we can see the symptoms of the schizophrenia which undoubtedly had an effect throughout his life. A surprising number of historical personages have been afflicted by either this disease or its closely allied complaint of manic depression. These diseases affected the work of writers, artists, composers and others, and in some cases influenced the course of history. Price was one of a distinguished company.

Whether he heard the 'voices' typical of schizophrenia we do not know, but one of his delusions is well recorded. It manifested itself when he visited the famous Rocking Stone on Pontypridd Common. This is a relic of unknown origin but there is a popular belief that it had some connection with the ancient Druids. In fact, any large or oddly-shaped stone lying about in Wales is sure to have a Druidic myth attached to it!

Price decided that he was himself an hereditary Archdruid, and he wrote out an astonishing affidavit of 725 folios which he deposited with the Public Records Office and in which he claimed to trace his inherited right to the local Ruperra Estate which he said had always belonged to the Druids.

He was soon incurring the anger of the local clergy by declaring that 'Man is greater that your God, for Man created God in his own image.'

This kind of thing did not go down well in a God-fearing, Chapel-going community. In an earlier age he would have been burned at the stake for such comments, and there were some who expressed the opinion that it was a pity burning had been abolished.

In a letter to a friend he wrote of the priests that 'They are paid to teach that the world of thieves and oppressors, of landlords and coal-owners, is a just world. Their theology is always that of the doctrine that the powers that be are ordained by God.'

A number of sermons were preached against him, but these were mild compared with the thundering denunciations that his activities in later years were to invoke.

1836 saw the beginning of the Chartist movement in London. The preamble to the Charter for adult male suffrage, regular elections, a salary for members of Parliament and the removal of property qualifications along with the introduction of other rights and freedoms, stated, 'We must draw into one bond of unity the intelligent and influential portion of the working classes in town and country, to seek by every legal means to place all classes of society in possession of their equal political and social rights, and to use every exertion to remove those cruel laws that prevent the free circulation of thought through the medium of a cheap and honest press.'

The preamble went on to mention the necessity to educate the masses so that they would know how to create a new civilisation in which they would no longer be governed by those 'who rule to their own advantage and not to ours'.

This latter aspect of the Charter doomed it from the start. The ruling classes were unlikely to help the masses to become so much better educated that they would in time be able to overthrow those who ruled them! The founders of the Charter were well meaning but naive bourgeois socialists of the Owenite school.

The ideals and aims of the Charter certainly appealed to the revolutionary soul of William Price. He, no more than the founders, could see the self-destruct element built into the preamble.

Local sections of the Charter were formed all over Britain, and Price was invited to a meeting held secretly somewhere near Pontypridd. It is unlikely that the organisers would have dared to try to hire any public hall, so it is almost certain that the gathering was held outdoors, possibly on Pontypridd Common, with flickering lanterns illuminating the scene, and everyone buoyed up by the excitement of knowing that they were defying 'them'.

In his speech to the meeting Price declaimed:

'We have tolerated the tyranny of those who oppress us – landlords, coal-owners, and the clergy – too long. We must strike with all our might and power. Let cowards go their way, for they have no part to play in this great struggle. Men of the valleys, remember that the principle behind Chartism is the principle which acknowledges the right of every man who toils to the fruits of his labours. The points embedded in this charter are our immediate demands. But ultimately we shall demand more. Oppression, injustice and the grinding poverty which burdens our lives must be abolished for all time. We are the descendants of valiant Welshmen and we must be worthy of the traditions which they have passed on to us.'

It was heady, revolutionary stuff, calculated to chill the blood of any landlord or coal owner. After a thunderous ovation he was elected leader of the Pontypridd and district section of the Charter. Such a meeting, attended by several hundred men – women played little part in such events except to support their men – would have had no chance of being kept quiet. The authorities undoubtedly had their spies in the crowd, and garbled versions of the doctor's speech gave him a high place on the police black list, Sir Robert Peel having formed the first civil police force (the Peelers) a few years previously.

After the meeting Price joined several of the leading spirits in a Llantrisant pub. He had moved from Nantgarw about this time. Those present included William Jones, a journeyman watchmaker; and John Frost, a draper. 'It is violent some of our masters are,' said Frost. 'When the time comes they will fight rather than give us our rights. We must be ready to fight, too.'

In the next century, Lenin was to say much the same. But John Frost was no Lenin.

'I agree,' said Price. 'The people must be ready to fight, but only if we are attacked first.'

'Sometimes,' Jones muttered, 'you have to strike before they hit you. Specially if they be stronger than you.'

In the months that followed, the Chartists were raising the Great Petition all over the country, and on July 12, 1839, the 1½ million signatures were presented to Parliament. The result of the debate that followed was rejection of the Charter by 235 votes to 46. The great landowners and capitalists of the new industrial age had seen the dangers and taken fright.

The founders of the Charter determined to carry on striving 'by every legal means' to achieve their goal but, as in any such movement, the militant fringe was prepared to resort to violence for revolution today, not in some vague tomorrow.

Frost and Jones were among the militants, and a plot was hatched to seize the town of Newport by force and set up what today would be called a people's republic.

Inevitably, the plot was given away, and when the conspirators led 4000 men armed with muskets, pikes and clubs into Newport they walked into an ambush. Frost and Jones were arrested and a warrant issued for Dr William Price, of which he was warned in time.

A favourite story is that, disguised as a woman, he walked onto a ship at Cardiff docks, and was helped up the gangplank by a police inspector placed there to look for him!

A few days later William Price arrived in Paris, to begin the first of his two French exiles, and to make his fateful acquaintance with the strange 'portrait of the primitive bard' in the Louvre.

Chapter 2

First Exile

November 6, 1839. William Price stood in the Place de la Concorde. The *diligence* from Calais had deposited him some distance from here but he had walked to this important spot before seeking lodgings.

It was raining: fine, incessant needles of rain, but he did not care. He revelled in the drama of the crowds and the sounds of a foreign tongue. He had learned some French at the Royal College of Surgeons along with the Latin, and expected to pick it up quickly.

This was where it had all happened, half a century ago. The people had risen against the oppressor class and claimed their own. Price was not a bloodthirsty man, and knew that he could not have approved if he had seen the blooded heads tumbling into the baskets, but his romantic nature, the essence of the Celt in him, thrilled to the vision of the *people*, banners flying in the wind as they sought their freedom.

He was wet, and it was cold. Necessity triumphed over history, and he went in search of an inn in the Montparnasse district.

He had a fair amount of money and had no doubt that he would be able to set himself up in medical practice, but he needed to make contacts and there was one possibility: a doctor friend, an Englishman, of his college days had married a French girl and gone to live in Paris because the bride's father had offered him a medical post.

He found an inn which was not very clean, and a landlord whom Price considered a rascal to charge so much for so little. It was not, he discovered, the habit of French inns to provide breakfast with your lodging, so, after rising he went out and found an excellent eating place which put him in a good mood.

The sun had come out, as if to apologise for its error of yesterday in having let Paris greet him under a cloud. He obtained directions and found his way to the last address that he had of John Masklyn, where his friend received him warmly.

'I knew that you would prove too troublesome for Wales to put up with you for long, William. You surely did not think that your armed rabble could overthrow the government in London and the big landowners. It is not that easy.'

Price shrugged philosophically. 'One does not always succeed the first time. Our day will come.'

Masklyn laughed. 'You are an idealist. But you cannot change humanity. Look what happened here. They chopped off the heads of the aristocrats then they fell out and chopped each other. Afterwards came Napoleon. He brought back the priests who had been expelled and he reopened the churches because he said the people needed religion. Then came Waterloo and the Bourbons returned. Everything is much the same as it was before they all started shouting for liberty, equality and fraternity.'

'I will argue with you some other time. Now I need your help. I have to earn some money. How do I go about starting a practice?'

John explained the procedure, and Price found him very helpful. Within a week he was installed in an apartment and had hung out his plate. It seemed that there were few regulations and the French medical authorities accepted British qualifications.

He had a two-level apartment, with the living quarters upstairs and two rooms below which he could use as surgery and waiting room. At first he had to hire a young man to sit with him and interpret with the patients, but by the end of a month, with his remarkable facility for language and his quick ear, he had mastered sufficient French to manage on his own. Masklyn had given him the address of a supplier of leeches and there was an apothecary nearby. Price's methods of treatment soon aroused comment, and he began to attract patients from more conventional doctors who had failed to cure their ailments. He did not believe very much in the use of leeches, and not at all in the prevailing fashion of 'purging'.

The Paris of 1839 in which William Price found himself bore no resemblance to the city that we know today. The Prefect Hausmann was not to begin for another fourteen years his gigantic task of driving the great tree-lined boulevards through the old city. Much of Paris in 1839 was a vast sprawl of narrow crooked streets and little courtyards, but there were also some grandiose buildings and pleasant open spaces. Besides the vast expanse of the Concorde there was the Place du Chatelet with its impressive Palm Tree Fountain. The Pont de la Revolution spanned the Seine in grandeur with its huge carved figures on pedestals, and the Porte St Denis opened onto an avenue wide enough to turn a coach and four round in it. The Arc de Triomphe, built by Napoleon to

18

celebrate his victories, towered over the houses and tenements.

In his spare time Price explored his place of exile. He climbed to the summit of the city's highest point: the hill of Montmartre, crowned by several windmills. Here, as he was to observe in warm weather, pretty girls in various stages of undress would emerge in the mornings from the lopsided houses to pick herbs or vegetables from sweet-smelling gardens.

Montmartre was the centre of Bohemianism and, left to himself, Price would have chosen to settle there, but he needed a more respectable district for his practice in order to attract patients who could pay a good fee.

He noted that students of the Latin Quarter had adopted a fashion of wearing hats in a variety of gay colours. This appealed to his inclination towards ostentation and he bought several. He also still wore his hair in two long plaits, which aroused some interest.

He visited Notre Dame and admired the great rose window; despite his antipathy to priests and all their doings he could nevertheless admire the splendours of Gothic architecture. He journeyed out to Versailles and walked in the gardens amidst the fountains, looked at the staterooms which Napoleon had had refurnished after the Revolutionary mob had originally looted the palace.

Sometimes letters came from Llantrisant. Frost and Jones had been transported. The Chartists had settled for pursuing their aims in democratic fashion. But the warrant for the arrest of William Price was still in force.

One day Price called on John Masklyn. 'You need to get to know people,' said John. 'Listen, I have been invited with my wife to a salon, what I suppose in England would be called a social evening. There will be wine and food and some people will play music and perhaps sing.'

'It sounds like a *noson lawen*, an evening of song and music that we have in Wales.'

'Whatever you call it, I am sure you will enjoy the experience. The invitation is from a Captain Phelps who is a friend of my wife's father, and I can take an extra guest along. The captain claims to be a brother-in-law to the King, Louis Philippe; though whether that is true I'm not sure. Anyway, he seems to have plenty of money and holds some splendid salons. He also has a very beautiful 17-year-old daughter.'

That evening at the house of Captain Phelps was to open some useful social doors for William Price, and also lead to a very embarrassing situation.

The villa was splendidly appointed, with a host of servants to wait on about 40 guests. Masklyn introduced his friend to their host, a man of about 45, tall with a military stance and the wearer of an impressive moustache so finely waxed and trained that it constituted a minor work of art. He greeted Price warmly. 'I have heard of Wales. I am told that you have some fine poets, although I cannot say I read any myself.'

'We have good voices, too,' said Price. 'But I do not share that national characteristic,' he added hastily, to forestall any possible invitation to sing.

'Allow me to introduce my daughter, Yvonne,' said Phelps, as the girl in the swirling yellow crinoline approached. Her dress was of the material called *foulard*, a thin mixture of silk and cotton so light that it revealed the promontories and bays of female geography to an extent that would have been indecent in Welsh society.

Price kissed her hand in courtly gesture. '*Enchanté, Mademoiselle.*' He looked into a pair of sea-green eyes with a lovely oval face like a cameo, framed by ringlets of corn-silk hair. What she saw was a tall, broad-shouldered man, looking younger even than his 39 years with those curious pigtails; healthy with the splendid bridge of a Welsh nose firmly set in a young-old face. She liked what she saw. And in her eyes Price recognised the flickering of a flame. He had not had a lot to do with the opposite sex apart from certain adventures during his college days in London, but he had seen that light before when they had looked at the young medic with the lilting Welsh voice.

'What are you doing in Paris, monsieur?' Her voice was soft, like a summer leaf fall.

'I am a doctor. I heal bodies.'

'Are you a famous doctor?'

'Not yet, but I will be the most famous of them all.'

Her sultry laugh was almost a caress.

The evening revealed that Yvonne had all the accomplishments of a young lady of her class. She took part in the musical offerings, playing the piano for an elderly baritone, and then delivering a couple of songs in a pleasant if untrained voice.

Price watched her move about the room, and thought that she was too young to have such a provocatively dangerous figure.

At the close of the evening as he bade farewell to his host, the Captain said, 'You must come and have lunch with us one day, Doctor Price. I will see that you receive an invitation.'

Price did not take him seriously, believing that it was one of those open invitations that people often issued without any intention of ever following it up. He was pleasantly surprised three weeks later to receive a card requesting his presence to lunch at the villa.

There were half a dozen guests, including Yvonne. He gathered that there was no current Madame Phelps. Throughout the meal he made full use of the charm that he knew well how to switch on. His French was now very fluent and he poured into that language all the Welsh eloquence that he could muster. He told them tall tales of an exciting life in a very glamorised version of his homeland and of his successes as a doctor.

For a prosperous middle class French audience he left out the slag heaps that blackened the countryside of south Wales for miles around the collieries, the hills of rubble from the slate quarries; they saw only a smiling land of yeomen farmers and contented villagers, and above all they learned of the superiority of Dr Price's medical treatments.

Captain Phelps was certainly intrigued, as was Yvonne. Afterwards the Captain led his new guest outside for a stroll in the garden.

'There are several friends of mine who have various ailments for which their doctors seem to have no cure. Perhaps I might suggest that they consult you.'

Price said that he would be most pleased to treat the Captain's friends.

Over the next few months his practice increased considerably as the Captain's referrals appeared at his surgery. Since they were all well off he had no scruples about charging them high fees. He was now able to indulge in the purchase of a pony and trap which enabled him to travel further when visiting patients. He also took on a young assistant doctor.

Several more invitations to the villa came his way; sometimes to lunch, sometimes to evening salons. He found that Yvonne had a lively intelligence and quick wit. He would liked to have been able to talk to her alone, but the opportunity did not arise.

One day Captain Phelps said, 'You should meet my friend Heinrich Heine. You could talk to him of philosophy and literature, and other scholarly matters. I will give you a letter of introduction.'

Price was interested. He had heard of the German writer and had in fact read in translation his *City of Lucca*, a book containing a section entitled *English Fragments* in which Heine proclaimed his moral allegiance to the principles of the French Revolution, at the same time severely criticising some anti-semitic writings of Cobbet's.

Phelps wrote the letter, and one afternoon Price drove his trap to an apartment in a fashionable district. A stout, middle-aged woman opened the door and took his card. He assumed that she was a servant, but learned later that the woman was some kind of companion to Mathilde, the barely-literate but good looking 20-year old Belgian shop girl whom

Heine had brought to live with him and whom he was later to marry.

Surprisingly, the Heine household never had a servant. Since Mathilde had no intellectual interest in his work, perhaps Heine thought that she might as well have domestic tasks to keep her busy.

The woman conducted him into a book-lined study where the famous philosopher, driven from Germany by political persecution, rose to meet him.

He read the few lines of Captain Phelp's letter, then extended a hand in greeting. 'I am pleased to make the acquaintance of a friend of Captain Phelps. Are you English?'

'No, Welsh.'

'Ah, I am pleased. I consider the English to be the most repulsive people that God in his wrath has ever created.'

'I belong to the most ancient race in Europe,' Price told him grandly. 'We were civilised when Rome was a village on the Tiber. I am myself descended from great bards of the past.' He was in one of his most extravagant moods.

'Indeed? You must tell me about this ancient race. Please be seated.' Heine brushed a hand across his classical features and ran heavy fingers through dark curly hair in a gesture that Price was to come to know well. The facial paralysis, precursor of the illness that was to kill him before his 60th birthday, had only just begun to affect him. Small in stature, only 5 feet 2 inches, he looked older than his 42 years.

They talked for a while, then Heine said, 'You must stay to lunch. We are having partridge. My Mathilde does a very good partridge. I will give you the recipe: you hang the bird in front of a good fire and let the juices drip onto a plate. Then into the juice you stir two eggs, mix together and pour over the partridge. It is very tasty.'

Price did indeed find Mathilde's partridge tasty, although in his apartment he kept to a strict vegetarian diet.

'You will find that Paris is awash with good restaurants,' Heine told him over the meal. 'After the Revolution all the good cooks who had served the aristos and the royal court were out of their jobs, so they started in business with their own places. You must visit the *Flicoteaux*. It has a front covered in little tiles overlooking the Place de la Sorbonne and you can dine well there for as little as sixteen sous. But if you want the mecca of gourmets you must go to *les Provencaux* where they do a marvellous *soles normandes*.'

Heine evidently appreciated good food, and the lunch was washed down with a bottle of Chateau Lafitte. He had come to Paris in 1830, and Alexander Dumas had said that since Germany did not want him, then France should adopt him.

That was the first of many visits that Price was to make to the home of Heinrich Heine. He came to enjoy discoursing with an intellectual equal on philosophy, the arts and the politics of the day.

One contact led to another. Captain Phelps had introduced him to Heine and it was the latter who was to give him a further and very useful contact that was to lend a new slant to Price's medical career.

'Have you ever heard of Doctor Christian Gottfried Samuel Hahnemann?' Heine asked one day.

'No, what does he do?'

'He is, like myself, a German exiled from his country, but he is not a literary man. He is a doctor of medicine with revolutionary ideas about disease and treatment. He makes very tiny tablets which he says give his patients a small dose of the disease from which they are suffering. Like cures like, so he says. It all sounds very peculiar to me, but I have heard of people who claim that he was cured them. I will write a letter if you would care to make his acquaintance.'

Price was immediately intrigued. Any medical man who had something new attracted him.

He found Dr Hahnemann in a large rambling old house, and Dr Hahnemann himself was large and rambling.

'What kind of a doctor are you, Monsieur Price? He looked severely over rimless glasses.

'Not the ordinary kind,' Price told him. 'I believe that most illness is caused by wrong living and eating. I do not purge or bleed, nor do I administer drugs that just ease the symptoms. I believe in natural food, as raw as possible. I am sure that we were never intended to eat meat but only the things that grow in the good earth. I believe that we should expose our bodies to the rays of the life-giving sun and to the rain, not keep them always shrouded in clothing.'

Dr Hahnemann surveyed his visitor with renewed respect, plainly recognising a kindred rebel. 'Come into my laboratory,' he invited.

In a long room at the top of the house he showed Price racks containing hundreds of labelled herbs, the ground up roots of plants, tree barks, even flowers, leaves, resins. Two assistants were busy at a bench with retorts, flasks, pestle and mortar.

'Let me explain,' Hahnemann spoke slowly, as Price discovered was his custom, as if allowing for lesser intellects to catch up.

'I believe that the human body has a great capacity for self-healing, and that the symptoms of a disease are the expression of the body's battle to overcome the disease. I have found that very minute doses of biological material will repeat the symptoms of a disease in an otherwise healthy body. Myself and my assistant have experimented on ourselves to prove this effect. If we give that substance, to an invalid it will cause the body to react by creating its own defences and will overcome the problem. Every individual is different and it is necessary to study the patient closely first to consider not only the symptoms but the whole person.'

Price rarely felt awed by another human being, his own ego was too great for that, but on this occasion he knew that he was in the presence of a great mind. As he came to know Hahnemann better, and to understand how utterly inflexible and autocratic the pioneer of homeopathy could be, the awe faded somewhat, but by then Price was embarked on his own experiments with the 'minimal dose'.

'Did you discover this all by yourself?' he asked.

Hahnemann smiled. 'I cannot claim that. The principle of 'let like be treated with like' was spoken of by physicians and alchemists in the seventeenth century. But it was known even earlier by Hippocrates himself. I call it homeopathy from the Greek, meaning 'like'.'

Soon after that first meeting, Price began to buy homeopathic remedies from Dr Hahnemann to try on his own patients. He also met the doctor's good-looking wife, Melanie and, though she was friendly, he was wary of her after Heine told him how the two came to be married.

'She came to his house in Leipzig where he was lecturing at the university and working in the homeopathic hospital that he had founded. She dressed like a man, in trousers. She has some of the characteristics of the famous George Sand of whom you have probably heard, the friend of the composer Chopin. I have met Madame Sand and I can testify that both she and Melanie Hahnemann are very determined ladies.'

'So how did they marry?' Price asked.

'She had heard of the great doctor and it seems had decided that he would propose marriage, and it was not long before he did. He had been married before but his wife had died and he was attended by two daughters in their teens. Before the wedding, Melanie wrote and signed an agreement that she would not accept any money from his will nor expect even to be mentioned in it. But a week after the wedding she had banished the daughters from the house and two months later she made him write a will leaving everything to her. He is a great doctor but feeble in the hands of that woman. Her next step was to make him move to Paris because this is where she had decided to live. Now she ensures that he treats only wealthy patients and charges high fees.'

From there on, Price took care to exert his Celtic charm on Melanie, a still handsome woman, tall and dark haired. She seemed, after the first meetings, to respond to him and after a while it was she who invited him to dinner one evening. Hahnemann had made no move to do more than talk to him on medical matters, but it was plain enough, as Heine had said, that she ran the household and the doctor did as she wished.

Price soon discovered that, not only did Melanie determine her husband's social life, but she also took a keen interest in medical affairs and discussed cases with him. Often he accepted her opinions on diagnosis and treatment, a situation which Price regarded as appalling.

Although not artistic or literary, like George Sands with whom Heine had compared her, she had friends in the Louvre, and suggested to Price that he would find a visit there very educational. He said that he would go, and the occasion of his going to the Louvre was to have a profound effect on the rest of his life.

But before that happening, his relations with Yvonne took a new turn. He had been invited to another of the Captain's lunches, and afterwards Yvonne offered to show him the rose garden that the Captain had recently laid out.

They strolled down the winding path. 'Have you seen much of our beautiful countryside, Doctor Price?'

He admitted that he had not. The villa was on the outskirts of the city and all around was rich farmland interspersed with forested areas.

'You must see what France is really like. Paris is not France. If you would like to come here on Saturday afternoon I would take you out in my carriage and show you the country.'

He accepted the invitation, and on the Saturday afternoon when he arrived she was waiting for him with a luxurious cabriole standing in the driveway, its brasswork shining in the sun and the liveried coachman sitting behind two sleek horses.

Captain Phelps was also standing by, obviously approving of his daughter's intention.

It was a pleasurable drive. The girl was well read and they discussed French literature: Balzac and Haussmann. Price told her of the bards of Wales, of the Eisteddfod and of the Mabinogion. She appeared to be fascinated.

Returning, she said, 'Have you been to the *Café d'Orsay*?'

He said he had not.

'It is very fashionable. We will have lunch there one day.'

He said he would like that.

Back at the villa there was coffee and cakes with an unusually jovial Captain Phelps. Nothing was said about the suggestion of lunch at the

Café d'Orsay, so Price stayed quiet, not being sure whether the Captain was supposed to know or not.

A few days later she sent him a note, and they met at the *d'Orsay*. He reflected that this could not have happened in England or Wales. No respectable 17-year-old girl could possibly have gone to lunch in a restaurant with a man and no chaperone. But, as he had already observed, social customs were free in Paris in 1840.

Yvonne proved to be no mere nibbler where food was concerned, and he wondered how much of that curvaceous figure would be left in a few years. She devoured a crayfish bisque followed by beef in Madeira with vegetables and finished with a vanilla soufflé.

She also drank more than her share of the bottle of Chablis that he ordered. She was a lively companion, commenting wittily on the other diners, many of whom, he gathered, had some degree of notoriety in Parisian Society. The wine sparkled in her eyes as he escorted her to her carriage.

'*Au revoir*,' she said with a giggle. 'My darling Welshman!'

The situation progressed from there on. A week later, at her suggestion, they met and enjoyed an evening at the *Comédie Francaise*. Afterwards, he took the opportunity of kissing her as they walked along the dimly lit street towards her carriage. She responded by pressing her body against him.

'We must take another ride in the country,' she said. 'There is a wood I know where we can walk – and be alone.'

He said it would be marvellous, and wondered how well did Captain Phelps know his daughter.

A week later they took another drive. It was a hot day. The countryside was lush and green. The horses trotted along a road lined with trees, on one side peasant farms, on the other, presently, a wood.

'*Arretêz-vous ici, s'il vous pláit*,' said Yvonne.

The driver brought the carriage to a stop beneath a tree. 'We will take a walk.' She stepped lightly onto the grass.

A path led through the trees and Price followed. 'This is a very quiet place,' she added.

In a few hundred yards they emerged into a sun-dappled glade. Yvonne folded her parasol with an almost defiant gesture, and flung it to the ground, following it with her bonnet. She then seated herself on the grass. Price joined her. In a moment she lay back as he kissed her.

He began slowly to unfasten the top of her dress, stoking the fire within her to furnace brightness.

'You are the lost loveliness that all men seek, the nameless desire that haunts the ragged edges of our dreams,' he murmured. His voice, speaking French with that heavy Welsh accent had always fascinated her from their first meeting.

She giggled, 'Which of your Welsh poets wrote those words?'

'I will tell you – William Price, bard of a thousand eisteddfodau.'

She purred like a kitten as he bared her to the waist. He kissed a nipple like the bud of a wild cherry sprouting from the whiteness and richness of a skin too much like milk ever to have seen the sun. He fumbled with the complex fastenings of her skirts and when his hands firmly but gently parted her satiny thighs to reveal the gateway of his needs, she wrapped her arms tightly round him and very soon showed that he was by no means the first to 'walk in the woods' with the daughter of Captain Phelps.

Neither of them heard a slight rustling of the bushes as the silent watcher stole away.

It was later than usual when they returned to the villa. They went first into the smaller of the two dining rooms the windows of which overlooked the driveway where the coachman had left the carriage standing. Normally the man would have been unharnessing the horses, but this time he had followed Price and Yvonne into the house and gone into the library where Captain Phelps was usually to be found at this hour.

A maid came in bearing the coffee pot. Price seated himself at the table and Yvonne went upstairs to attend to her toilette. The maid placed the pot on the table and went out. Through the window Price saw the coachman emerge and begin to attend to his horses.

A moment later the door crashed open and Captain Phelps erupted into the room. An angry red was creeping out of his collar and he appeared to be on the verge of choking.

'Monsieur, you are a villain and a scoundrel, a despoiler of women. I gave you my friendship, the hospitality of my home. I trusted you with my daughter and you have debauched her. If it were not that duelling is forbidden in France I would call you out at tomorrow's dawn. Go from my house!'

Price rose with as much dignity as he could muster and walked to the door.

'Go! Go!' the Captain thundered, pointing a dramatic finger that quivered with fury.

As Price drove away in his trap he reflected that it was a somewhat unfortunate situation. He refused to use the word embarrassing even to himself. His ego would not allow him to do so. 'What did the man

27

expect?' he said to the trotting horse. 'He threw his daughter at me. Marriage I suppose he wanted. But marriage is not for me.'

He did worry, however, for some weeks, as to whether the Captain might take some legal action against him, not being aware of the state of French law in such matters, and he could hardly say to anyone, 'I have just violated the daughter of Captain Phelps. Do you think there might be any consequence?' But nothing happened, and he never saw or heard of the Captain or Yvonne again.

Life continued as before. The parting from Phelps did his practice no harm. His treatments were becoming too well known for that. He experienced increasing success with the homeopathic remedies, or, at least enough to convince him that they did work, that there was something in the theory that like could cure like.

It was on a day in the autumn that he decided to take an afternoon off and go to the Louvre as Melanie Hahnemann had suggested.

He wandered through the many galleries of the vast treasure palace that the last king of France had planned and the Revolutionary Government had inaugurated, but it was the antiquaries that attracted him, and eventually he came to a room containing archaeological discoveries dating from BC.

He had been feeling restless for some days, wondering if he would ever see his homeland again. He had also been having strange dreams of a repetitive nature. In these he was always lost in a big city, frantically seeking a road out to Llantrisant but never finding it. Strangers whom he approached had never heard of the place and always the roads ran far ahead, unfamiliar, endless, but he kept on walking, hoping for a sign that would take him to the village.

As he walked through the galleries he was also bothered by a headache that he had had for some days. He had been taking the homeopathic remedy cinchona, but with only limited relief.

He came to a glass case in which there reposed a curious oval yellow stone, about 10 inches by 8 at its widest. It was not a perfect oval, having been roughly cut. There was a sun symbol in the centre and along the radiating rays some kind of hieroglyphics had been carved. A label stated that the stone had been found at Carnac, in Brittany. Price had read of the hundreds of standing stones in the fields there that had puzzled all the learned men who had studied them. Many were of the dolman type familiar at Stonehenge. It was impossible to guess at their origin. The label added that no one had ever deciphered the markings on the oval stone.

Price felt a sudden throbbing in his head, and a voice seemed to say

28

'you have been chosen'. In a dazzling flash of revelation he knew what was meant. The hieroglyphics spelt it all – he, William Price, was the direct descendent of a high priest of all the druids of long ago, of the mystic cult that had made the stones of Carnac, of Stonehenge and of all those mysterious circles of stones scattered across Wales.

He knew now that the druids of 4000 years ago would guide him to rescue the old order that had flowered in the morning of the world, before even Pan had played his pipes on the slopes of Olympus. The druids were old, old, the guardians of the true wisdom that had yet to be revealed to mankind. And he, William Price, was of them.

He pulled a notebook from his pocket and hastily copied the hieroglyphics. He never remembered leaving the Louvre, but he was back in his apartment, drinking a lot of black coffee, his face beaded with sweat. He fell asleep. He also felt a renewed confidence in himself and a sense of destiny.

He took the notebook to Heine, who removed his glasses and stared at his visitor in astonishment. 'You can read these marks? How?'

'I have learned the script of the druids,' replied Price casually, and he believed it.

'And these marks tell you that you are a descendant of the high priest of some four thousand years ago?'

'That is so. It is my duty and my destiny to bring back the faith of the druids.'

Heine weighed his words carefully, as if they were gold coins to be spent one at a time. 'Do you not think, my friend, that you are devoting too much time to your patients? That perhaps you should rest?'

Price laughed, the sound deep in his broad chest. 'You think I am mad? I will show you. I will show them all that I am a man with vision.'

He departed, walking with a light step. He had no more dreams, though, and he never mentioned the stone again while he was in Paris. But this episode, arising from his latent schizophrenia, was to remain with him for the rest of his life. The illusion that he was being used by long gone druids was to colour much of his future activity.

Chapter 3

Megan

Back in Wales, he took up residence in the parish of Eglwysllan, near Pontypridd, and resumed what was for him normal life. That is to say he soon worked up a vigorous medical practice, aided by a flow of homeopathic tablets from Hahnemann in Paris, got himself involved in several court cases through suing those unwise enough to cross his path, and continued to infuriate the clergy and fellow members of his profession with his opinions, given either in public lectures (often rowdy occasions) or in articles in the local press.

In 1848 Megan Evans came into his life. Price was called to the farm of Evan Evans, and he was not surprised to find the farmer groaning on his bed with pain and clutching his stomach. This had happened several times before and Prince had no doubt about the cause. Evans was spending far too much time in the local pubs.

He shook his head with a sad expression. 'It is indeed a bad way you are in, Mr Evans. Serious it is.'

The farmer paled. 'Help me, Doctor Price. You are a clever man. Everyone says so.'

'I will do my best. I will be back in a moment.'

Price went downstairs from the bedroom to the big farmhouse kitchen where Evans' daughter, 21-year-old Megan, was busy at the wood-burning range. Evans was a widower with two grown-up sons and Megan.

He had seen the girl two or three times on visits to the father, and had noted with appreciation the sway of her shapely body which could not be quite hidden by the simple peasant dress. He liked tall women. As he entered, she brushed one forearm across her forehead in a gesture that he was to come to know well, almost displacing her bonnet.

'I saw a pond out there by your vegetable patch. Are there frogs in it?'

'Why, yes, Doctor Price, sir. We do have a few frogs.'

'I want you to take a jug and see if you can catch one for me. It is for a little experiment I am going to do that I hope may cure your father and

I want you to help me, but he is not to know. It must be our secret.'

Her grey eyes sparkled at the thought of helping and sharing a secret with the good-looking Dr Price. Abandoning the dish she was stirring, Megan grabbed a jug from the great Welsh dresser and hastened outside.

Presently she came back with a frog. Price took it upstairs, being careful to conceal the jug behind the farmer's bed where the man, being too engrossed with his pain, would be unlikely to see it. Then he took a powder from his bag.

'Take this, Mr Evans. It will soon cure your stomach ache.'

Evans gratefully took the powder with a drink of water, and in a few minutes vomited into a bucket which Price had also borrowed from the kitchen. The powder had been a harmless emetic. As Evans lay back groaning on his bed. Price quickly reached for the jug and dropped the frog into the bucket.

'Look, man; that is what was causing your pain!'

Evans gazed with horror at the frog swimming in the bucket.

'That was inside you,' said Price gravely.

'My God, doctor! That is terrible! I never knew such a thing was possible. Indeed I owe you my life. But am I cured for good?'

Price shook his head. 'No, because it will have left some baby frogs inside, and they will grow.'

'What must I do? How can I get rid of them?'

'They feed on beer. Nothing else satisfies them. Without it they die. Only if you stop drinking entirely will you be free of the frogs.'

Evans swore that he would never go to a public house again. Never! Ever!

'You have taught me a lesson, Doctor Price. Indeed you have. I drink only God's own water from now on.'

'Good man,' said Price, patting his patient on the shoulder. 'I will be sending you my bill.'

He went down to the kitchen. 'Your father is much better now, and he will be all right so long as he stays out of public houses.'

'I am very glad, doctor. Isn't it the ale he needs to be off, I know.'

He observed that, since he went upstairs she had changed her garments and now wore a quilted petticoat of lavender satin and a *bedgwn* of dark blue. She had also just put on a shawl of yellow with red and green patterning, and was apparently ready to go out.

'Would you be kind enough to take me into the village, Doctor Price? I wish to buy some things at the shop and it will save time.'

She picked up a basket and sat beside him on the journey, chatting inconsequentially. The nearness of the girl, the jolting of the carriage on the rutted lane pushing her body often against him, was disturbing. Price had been celibate for all of the three years since his return, and had lately begun to feel the need for some feminine company in the house-cum-surgery where he lived alone but for the daily visits of his housekeeper.

Megan had the allure of youth, a healthy tanned skin that came from working in the fields, and the folds of her clothing could not conceal the swell of her breasts.

The village was small, offering only the general store and the Red Lion. 'When you have finished your purchases,' he said. 'Would you like to eat with me? It is time for my lunch before I continue my rounds.'

Her eyes glowed as she turned her face towards him. 'Indeed I would like that, doctor.'

He watched her walk away towards the shop. He had always liked tall young women.

She joined him presently in the pub, having filled her basket. Price had a pint of Welsh ale and Megan asked for milk. He ordered roast potatoes, bread and butter and cheese, for which he considered sixpence to be a reasonable charge, although he sighed – not for the first time – for the restaurants of Paris.

'You will be doing all the work in the house since your mother died,' he said. 'Are you not thinking of marrying?'

She frowned. 'I do not like any of the boys here and, anyway, I will not be doing all the work alone for very long. My father is taken with a new woman. She is Mary Jones of Pontypridd. She does not please me.'

'That will be unfortunate. Maybe I will be able to think of something for you.'

She sparkled, and her smile lit the dingy pub. 'That would be nice. I will be very grateful, doctor. Very grateful.'

He thought about Megan often in the next few days, and then it so happened that he had to visit the Evans farm again, not for the father. Evans, from what he heard, had taken his fright to heart and had not been seen in the Red Lion since, but one of the sons had a badly gashed leg from an accident in the haymaking.

Price dressed the wound, and was amused, just when he was leaving, the same thing happened as before. Megan asked him to take her into the village.

'Have you thought of anything for me, Doctor Price?'

'Yes, I have. I am greatly taken by you, Megan. How would you like to come and live with me at my house? We would be as man and wife, but there will be no wedding, you understand? I do not agree with marriage. You are able to read, you could keep my books for me, make appointments for my patients and care for the house. And you would be company for me. What do you say?'

Her gaze met his in a direct and challenging way, and her pink tongue flicked out to wet her lips. She said simply: I would like that very much. But what will my father say?'

'Leave your father to me. I will talk to him and tell him that the choice is freely yours.'

He took her to the village, leaving her there to shop. She would walk back to the farm. Country girls were used to walking.

The next day, he came again to the Evans homestead. The farmer was milking one of his cows, but stopped and wiped his hands as he saw the doctor approaching.

'I would talk with you, farmer Evans. Shall we go into the house?'

'Sure, sure, doctor. I have been all right since your treatment, and I do not go now to the Red Lion.'

'Fine, fine.' In the living room, Price refused the offer of a pot of tea. 'I want your daughter, Megan, to come and live with me. She says that she would like to do so. She is a bright girl. She will cook and keep my house and my books. I am told you are marrying again, so you will not miss her help so much.'

'Indeed that is so. Mary Jones of Pontypridd has agreed to be my wife. But, you mean for my Megan to live in your house?'

'That is what I said. It is all of ten miles from here. Would you have the girl walk home every night?'

'No, no. But what will people think – a young girl and a single man in the same house?'

Price looked at him with amusement. 'Why, man, they will think that we will be sharing a bed together, and of course we will. Your daughter will be my mate. That is the way of nature, the male and the female seek each other for the purpose of mating. You are a farmer. What do your animals do?'

Evans raised a hand to ruffle his thinning hair in bewilderment. 'But will you not marry her?'

'Marry! Do you not know my views on marriage? It is the woman's prison. Men and women should be free to live together as they wish, without all that hocus pocus of church or chapel. The giving away as if the father owned the daughter, the vows that human weakness cannot always keep. That is not for me. Your daughter has chosen of her own free will to agree to live with me. You have no right to hold her. I merely do you the courtesy of coming to tell you what is decided.'

'Hold on a minute, doctor,' the baffled farmer protested. 'The girl is worth something. Could we not have some agreement, something to make it worth while for me to lose her?'

Price drew himself up to his full six feet. 'Farmer Evans! You would sell your daughter! I do not buy women like you buy cattle. She is a woman, twenty one years of age, a free citizen making a free choice, not for sale.'

'Well, of course, doctor; you are right. Indeed you are. I cannot sell my daughter, but, look you, I must get advice. I will talk to the Reverend Jones at the chapel.'

'Very well. I do not wish to come between father and daughter, so I will wait a few days. But in the end, it is Megan's decision.'

He departed. Two days later, he was in his surgery having dealt with the last patient of the day, when Mrs Williams, his housekeeper, knocked to inform him that the Reverend Jones would like to see him. Sensing that this was no medical consultation, Price agreed to see his visitor.

The Reverend was a small man with a face like one seen in the back of a spoon. Price had heard of his sermons in which the man appeared to use the cross as a weapon with which to assail those of lesser faith, instead of as a guiding light.

'What is your problem, Reverend Jones? Gout troubling again?'

'No. 'tis not the gout, Doctor Price. I come on a more serious matter.'

Price looked at him with sardonic amusement. 'More serious than the gout? Then this must indeed be serious. I have heard patients say that gout is the very devil, if you Reverence will excuse me taking the name of your sworn enemy.'

'I am aware of the irreverence of your attitude to the faith, doctor, and I am even more distressed that you propose to corrupt a young girl by luring her away from her father to come and live in your house.'

'If you speak of Megan Evans of the farm, then I am aware of no corruption. Megan has made a free choice to share my home. That is her right as a free adult woman.'

'But her father tells me that you intend for you both to live together as man and wife, but without the holy sacrament of marriage. Is that so?'

Price weaved his eyebrows into a frown, as if puzzled by the question. 'Certainly. I question the so-called idealism and morality of your legalised monogamic marriage. It is no more than a property relationship. The bride is first the property of her father and is then *given* away at your altar like a sack of potatoes to another man, and she is expected to sink her own identity into his even to the extent of losing the name by which she was born. I would like to see marriage become a

34

union freely accepted, freely maintained, and freely dissolved if necessary by mutual consent. The community should intervene only in order to safeguard that which is of vital interest to it, namely: the children.'

'Heresy!' the reverend spluttered. Red was creeping up to his collar and he appeared to be rumbling inside like a frustrated volcano. 'Such views undermine the foundations on which the Christian family is based. What would happen to our civilisation if people just live together anyhow they chose?'

'I believe it will happen one day. Sometime in the future free love will replace the shackles of marriage. Lovers will live together to see how they get along before embarking upon any formalised legal union. And if they still find that they are unsuited, then the law will allow them to separate without fuss.'

'It will be a sad, sad day when that happens. And if it does, the devil will have triumphed. Children will be deprived of real family life.'

'Not so. Common-sense will have won. However, we must beg to differ there, since neither of us can see through the mists of the future. But meanwhile, Megan Evans has decided of her own free will. That is all. Good day, Reverend Jones.'

The following day, Price went again to the Evans farm. Megan was in the kitchen, looking somewhat hot and tearful. 'My father does not like it,' she said, 'but I have told him that I am coming to you. I will not stay here and be a slave for Mary Jones. I will not!'

'That is fine,' said Price, gently kissing her. 'You have made your own choice. I will talk to him.'

The farmer was in the living room. 'You have won, doctor. My Megan is a stubborn girl. She is determined to go and live with you, and the Reverend Jones says he can do nothing. But surely, doctor, some recompense is mine for losing my daughter's labour about the house and farm? She will be sorely missed. Indeed she will.'

Price relented. 'I will tell you what I will do, so that you will not feel too bereaved, shall we say – I will treat any of your ailments free of charge from now on.'

Evans brightened. 'That is indeed generous of you, Doctor Price. I am grateful – and my sons you will treat, too?'

Price scowled. 'You presume, sir, on my generosity.'

'They are healthy boys, doctor. Hardly anything ever wrong with them, just a scratch now and then.'

'All right, all right. You drive a hard bargain, farmer Evans. But I will treat your sons as well.'

'And my Mary, when she comes?'

'Certainly not! Your Mary will probably have a brood of brats and you would have me treat those also, and maybe their children – if I live long enough. Good day to you, sir. We have our bargain. That is all.'

He stamped out indignantly. The bargain was, however sealed. Two days later Megan Evans moved into the doctor's house, Mrs Williams being paid off. Megan took readily to her tasks as cook, housekeeper, book-keeper, receptionist for the patients. The Reverend Jones delivered a pointed sermon at the chapel concerning 'those among us who live in sin', but none dared tackle Dr Price on the subject.

In a public lecture he again assailed the medical profession, saying:

'Medical science has always believed in the superstition that poisons which are harmful and destructive to human life will prove an efficient substitute for the violation of natural laws. This money-making profession has always taught that mankind can be absolved from physical disease by prescribing a few pills, or injecting a poisonous vaccine or serum. We are suffering under the curse of the past mistakes of our profession. We have been educating the public into the false belief that poisonous drugs can give health. This belief has become such a deep-rooted superstition, that those of us who know better and who would like to adopt more rational methods, can only do so at the risk of losing our practice and reputation. The average doctor is at his best but a devoted bigot to this damnable teaching which we call the medical art, and which alone in this age of science, has made no perceptible progress since the days of its earliest teachers. Some call it recognised science, but I call it recognised ignorance!'

Many today would say that not a lot has changed, but the modern medical profession is even more obsessed with drugs that only suppress symptoms while failing to tackle causes.

Megan had been with him for some months when he was called upon to attend a miner whose left leg had been crushed in an accident underground. Price looked at the damage and knew that a section of the shin bone was too badly shattered ever to be able to knit. The leg would be useless and the man in permanent pain.

'Dafydd Williams,' he said. 'If you are willing to have an operation, I believe that I could replace that useless bone with a piece from the leg of a calf. It has not been done before. Are you willing to try it?'

Dafydd, in great pain, agreed, and preparations were made for the operation in a spare room in Price's house. Although Lister's work on germs, showing the necessity for strictly antiseptic conditions in operating rooms, was still some years in the future, Price seemed to know instinctly the need for hygienic conditions. He and Megan cleaned and scrubbed the entire room and he sterilised his instruments in boiling water.

Megan had already assisted him in minor operations and proved that she did not faint when the blood flowed.

Chloroform, invented by Simpson a few years earlier, had already reached South Wales, and this was used on the patient, administered by Megan.

Price showed that he was, indeed, a skilled surgeon, and the bits of shattered bone were cleared away to be replaced by the calf bone already shaped to fit.

Dafydd came round and a few days later seemed to be making good progress. But then, Price, called to find him running a fever.

The operation was a success – but the patient died. Unfortunately, Price could not know about the body's ability to reject any foreign matter. Drugs to suppress the immune system were far in the future.

Such a failure was a bitter blow to the doctor, and he never again attempted any kind of transplant.

The following year, Megan had a baby girl, christened Iarlles Morganwg. The child was later to accompany him in many of his court appearances, where she would sit at the barristers' table and be frequently addressed by her father as 'my learned counsel'.

About this time, some members of the medical profession thought they saw their chance to get back at their perennial critic by having him charged with manslaughter. Why they missed their chance of doing this on the occasion of the failed operation on Dafydd Williams is a mystery. Instead they chose to pick on the incident concerning a Thomas Price of Penydarreu, Merthyr. The doctor had received an urgent message to go and see him. He found the patient with a large swelling on one knee.

'You must stay in bed with that,' Price commanded. 'On no account leave your bed for several days.'

Two days later the man appeared at the surgery, having driven in a trap with his brother and two other men who carried him inside.

The knee had plainly become much worse, but after Price had removed an accumulation of fluid from beneath the skin, the patient was delighted to find that he could walk unaided.

'Do not think this cures you,' said Price. 'You must go home immediately and to bed for several days.'

Unfortunately, this advice was not followed. Thomas Price and his pals called at several public houses along the way, and it was five o'clock in the morning when they arrived home. The aftermath was a cold which brought on inflammation of the lungs from which he died.

At the inquest, three doctors of Merthyr swore that death had been the result of maltreatment by the doctor who had attended. A formal charge of manslaughter was brought against Price who immediately demanded that the body – which had been buried by then – be exhumed for post-mortem examination.

This required the permission of the Home Secretary in London, at that time a Mr Austin Bruce, who at first denied that he had any power to grant it. But Price, as well informed on the law as any lawyer, managed to convince the Home Secretary that he did have the power and that it should be used in this case.

The body was exhumed and examined in a local church by three independent doctors who confirmed that death was due to inflammation of the lungs. Despite this, the case was proceeded with. Price as usual, conducted his own flamboyant defence and the verdict was "not guilty".

Once again the giant had triumphed over the envious pygmies whom he saw as swarming round his feet, forever seeking to bring him down.

'You spoke marvellously,' said Megan, who had been in court.

'I live in a world of little men, but they cannot make ropes strong enough to bind or trap me.'

Chapter 4

Trial

As the child grew, so, in a different sense, did Megan. She took to reading many of the non-medical books in his library, of which he had many on a variety of subjects. Price encouraged the furthering of her education, seeing himself as a Pygmalion and Megan as the statue into which he was breathing life. Under his tuition, the mental horizons of the farm girl expanded and flowered. This blossoming was also eventually to take her away from him, but that he could not foresee.

The doctor took up a new passion: campaigning against the habit of smoking the 'devil's weed' which be became convinced was not only a dirty custom but was also harmful to health, even though of course he had no scientific proof of that.

On one occasion, after the railway line had opened between Merthyr and Pontypridd, he was travelling by train and asked a fellow passenger to stop smoking. The man refused, whereupon Price threw the clay pipe through the window and threatened that the offender would follow if he dared to complain.

In 1853 Price was accused of perjury in a complicated case which looked as if it might be his undoing.

The trial of the Queen versus William Price for perjury took place in Cardiff at the Glamorganshire Summer Assizes on July 18 and 19, 1853, before Her Majesty's Justice Baron Platt and the Jurors. The indictment reads:

> On the 11th of March, 1853, in the County Court, William Millward sought to recover damages against Ann Millward and Frederick Burns, her bailiff, for seizing his goods by virtue of a distress to rent. It became a material question whether William Price had instructed Frederick Burns and told him where to go to make the said distress, and had met him, and had seen him at Treforest on the 24th January, 1853. William Price, duly sworn, said

that he had not come for the bailiff, had not told the plaintiff where to go or what to do; had not met the bailiff at Treforest, and had not seen him at Treforest on the 24th January, 1853. Whereas, &c, he had come, &c, had told &c, had seen &c, had met &c, and so did commit wilful and corrupt perjury.

Some parts of the case are amusing and seem to almost resemble a cross-talk act. The official court records relate the following:

Cross-examined by Dr Price – Do you know your Christian name? (laughter) Witness: Robert Francis is the name I go by.

On Dr Price continuing to put questions relative to Mr Langley's Christian name, his Lordship addressing Mr Price said – 'You cannot expect a man to say I was present at my christening, and although I was then three weeks old I cannot remember them giving me a name. (laughter). It matters naught about the gentleman's name: If his name were Beelzebub he is a very good witness (renewed laughter).

Mr Price – Did you hear me give my evidence? Witness: I did.

Mr Price here began to examine witness as to the evidence he (Mr Langley) gave before the magistrates, when his Lordship said if Mr Price wished the witness to speak to the evidence he then gave, his deposition then taken must be read, and he cautioned Mr Price as to calling for that to be read, as that would give the counsel for the prosecution the right of making a second speech to the jury.

Mr Price insisted on having the deposition read, after which Mr Langley said Mr Bird asked Mr Price whether he was nominally or really the plaintiff (meaning the defendant) in the action to which Mr Price replied, I am not.

Mr Price (addressing his Lordship) here contended that Mr Langley could not know Mr Bird's meaning, and that his (Mr Price's) answer was the truth, and very material, for he could not by possibility be the plaintiff.

Mr Langley explained that Mr Bird must mean defendant, because the plaintiff in the action was William Millward, his own client.

The case continued in much the same confused manner with much 'laughter in court' for several pages of the official records. The highlight of the case, however, was undoubtedly Price's own peroration for the defence, a masterpiece of obfuscation and high flown rhetoric.

My Lord and Gentlemen of the Jury –

As my brain has been ploughed and harrowed for the last five months, and sown by the conspirators with the seeds of villainy and malice, I beg you will hear me patiently and with all the indulgence you can afford to an innocent victim of persecution, to mow down their harvest of perjury!

In obedience to the Throne, the inhabitants of my country, and the law of my land, I yield to no man as well as, in respect to the seat of judgement, wherein you sit on behalf of the Queen.

To enable you to understand my present position, hunted into this dock by the blood-hounds and their huntsmen, who took away my liberty, on the 4th day of April, 1853, *by perjuring themselves.*

I beg you will hear from me, patiently, the shortest possible account of the facts, circumstances, and connection of events, the *animus* of the how and the why I appear now before you to defend myself against a Charge of Perjury, that never had existence in *my* mind, nor in the *expression* of my mind, by the words of my mouth, on my oath, in Millward versus Millward on the 11th of March, 1853, before the Judge of the Small Debts' Court at Cardiff.

I think I shall be able to show to your satisfaction that this charge against me was born and bred in the brain of Thomas Falconer, Esq. and nourished by his influence over the conspirators, John Bird, Robert Francis Langley, Frederick Burns, John Hodkinson, and other greater and lesser lights in the background plot, for the express purpose of taking away my liberty, destroying my reputation and arresting my right course, because I have repeatedly refused to prostrate my senses in this court, and other places, to his dictation and their threatening of prosecution.

I believe my name is William Price. I am a medical man in a very extensive practice, residing near Ponty Priydh. I have been practising my profession in the same neighbourhood for more than 30 years. The late Thomas Millward and family were, and are still, except William Millward, the plaintiff, herein named, among some of my oldest patients.

During the last illness of the late Thomas Millward, I made his will, by his request and his dictation.

I attended the late Mary Millward, the widow of Thomas Millward, in her late illness. At her request and by her dictation, I made her will but, after delaying the execution of it to the last moment, she hesitated and refused to sign it, because she was afraid of *Billy*. This *Billy* is the plaintiff in Millward versus Millward. I do assure you, my Lord and Gentlemen of the Jury, it is not with pleasure, but it is with pain, my present position compels me to pull up the black soul of *Billy* from his mother's grave to show you the animus, the soul of this malicious, ex-officio prosecution against me, instituted at the suit of the Queen, as a banner to enlist similar souls to accomplish the ruin of his sister, Ann Millward, the defendant, in the inevitable ruination that awaits me, if you find me guilty of the false charge perjury levelled against my innocent heart by the conspirators, John Bird, Robert Francis Langley, Frederick Burns and others, under the influence and instigation of Thomas Falconer Esq. Nothing but the black soul, of this ex-officio prosecution, in the Queen's name against me, could induce me here publicly, before your Lordship, to impeach a functionary, in the administration of the Law of the land, who encourages the black soul of the plaintiff, to assist in Ann Millward, the supreme authority of the Church, to administer the property of her late parents, on her path under a heavy penalty, and who instigates these proceedings against me, to involve Ann Millward, the administratrix, and destitute defendant, and myself, in one common ruin.

The dying words of the late Mary Millward, the mother of the plaintiff and of the defendant, in the presence of her daughters, and in my presence, were, *Mae arno hi ofn Bily y o wneuthyr ngwyllhys.* I have offended Billy mortally by making his late father's will, protecting his aged mother in her widowhood from his insensibility and drunken hard-heartedness, and after her decease, for patronising the unsullied character of his orphan sister, Ann Millward, the defendant, in the plaint out of which this prosecution sprang, on the 11th of March, 1853, where I appeared as a witness for the defence, to an agreement made by me and Thomas Thomas of the Bridgewater Arms, Ponty Priydh, as peacemakers between and at the direction and request of both parties.

These proceedings in reply, by the instigation, advice and counsel of Mr Bird, could have had no other earthly object in view but to resist and delay the payment of the £100 rent, then due to Ann Millward by their agreement, to starve her into compliance to her brother's will, thereby tempting her to violate her oath, at Llandaff, as the administrator of her father's will where I had become one of her bail. Out of these acts of charity grows one of the horns of my dilemma.

The other horn is the ex-officio prosecution, generated in a conspiracy in the Small Debts' Court under the influence of Thomas Falconer, Esq., the Judge on the self same day of the 11th March, 1853, for exposing the extortion committed by his satellites,

Robert Francis Langley, Frederick Burns and others, in the Queen's name, under the seal of the court, by putting an execution into my house on the 1st of December, 1852, and plundering therefrom the sum of £5.11.4d which had been paid once by me before, as the receipt shows.

Let it be borne in mind, too, that the hearing of this complaint for extortion was the first business transacted by the judge on that day. Having tried in vain to excuse his satellites from this charge of extortion, I observed that his argument was not warranted by the written evidence of extortion before him. 'What!' said the judge, 'do you say no to me!'

'I do,' replied I, 'say no to you, sir, but not meaning it discourteously to the authority vested in you. The evidence of the receipts produced is beyond doubt.'

The judge called up Langley to explain away the evidence of the receipts which, he mumbled in some broken sentences I could not gather, to the satisfaction of the judge.

The effect of which was to warm his heart, to exculpate Langley by striking again at the evidence of my senses, by denying the evidence of the written documents.

This induced me to again say 'No sir,' to the judge. 'That is impossible! It is contrary to the evidence of the receipts, and the explanation of the transaction by the officer of the court, Frederick Burns, who signed the receipts and gave the explanation.'

'What?' asked the judge again with threatening countenance and malignant eye, 'do you say no to me?'

'Indeed, sir,' replied I, 'I do, without meaning any offence or discourtesy to the authority vested in you. There is no man living has a greater respect for that authority than I have. I charge the officers of your court for plundering me in the Queen's name, under their seal of office, of the sum of £5.11.4d.'

Robert Francis Langley then got up and threatened me with a prosecution if I dared to repeat the charge against him.

This is the same Robert Francis Langley that has given his evidence in this court today against me on behalf of the Crown, and the same Frederick Burns who signed the receipts.

Heedless of the consequences of his threatenings, and the scowling countenance and malignant eyes of Thomas Falconer, Esq., to back him, I repeated the same charge against that Robert Francis Langley, then assistant Clerk of the Small Debts' Court (that sainted villain who swears to my meaning, in this court today) for plundering me, in the Queen's name, under the seal of his office, of £5.11.4d upon which, the judge asked me what I wanted?

I replied, 'Sir, I want my money returned.'

The judge upon that, gave me leave to mention the circumstances to him next court.

Some two hours afterwards, on the same day, the Plaint of Millward versus Millward came off, in favour of the plaintiff, '*Billy ni*'.

Just as I was leaving the court, the judge addressed me, saying that if the dispute on the matter in difference was left to his adjudication, he would see justice done. I replied, as it was not my business, I could say nothing, that I had always advised the party for whom I appeared as witness that day, to have nothing to do with law and lawyers if she could possibly help it. And even if I did advise her to leave the matter in difference to his settlement, I knew the party had no faith in his justice.

In the course of three or four days afterwards, there came after me the Superintendent of the Cardiff Police from the Borough Magistrates, charging me with falsely, wickedly, wilfully, and corruptly, for having committed wilful and corrupt perjury in the Plaint of Millward versus Millward on the 11th day of March, 1853, commanding me to appear on 17th of that month at Cardiff before the Mayor. As commanded, I appeared on the 17th, and got the hearing of the charge postponed to the 4th of April, 1853, on which day I appeared there again to answer the trumped up charge against me, with the evidence of Ann Millward, the defendant in my defence, and attended then as now, by my infant daughter, Iarlles Morganwg as my learned counsel for the defence. When the case was called I begged the Mayor, William Williams Esq., for the ends of justice, he would be pleased to order all persons who are to be examined, for, and against me, out of the court, under the penalty of being objected to.

The Mayor, William Williams, Esq., in the name and on behalf of the Queen of Great Britain, nodded his assent, and forthwith ordered all persons to leave the court that were to be examined for, or against me, under the penalty of being objected to. I had obtained summonses signed by the Mayor to command the attendance of witnesses on my behalf in the Police Court that day. John Blys served John Bird in the court, in the presence of and in the sight of the Mayor of Cardiff.

What do you think, My Lord, and Gentlemen of the Jury, was

there and then done in contempt of the Queen's Authority, by the said John Bird, the attorney for the prosecution, in the sight and under the sanction of the representative of the Queen of Great Britain?

Why! It is almost incredible!

It is incredible, I believe, everywhere else in Great Britain, but in Cardiff and her lunatic asylums!

But, as facts are in Cardiff, like facts in everywhere else, I will dare tell you, and produce witnesses of the facts. This is what was said and done by one of the conspirators in infamy, John Bird, and gainsaid and undone by the Mayor of Cardiff, the representative of the Queen in the court on that day.

My Lord, and Gentlemen of the Jury! Observe their *animus*, in .this preliminary stage of the prosecution!

This blundering conspirator, John Bird, cocksure of his game, said, in the face of the court, that it was an unwarrantable act, and in contempt of court, to serve him with a summons. *He would not go out!*

He clearly proved by his act that he felt what he spoke, for once in his life, for he put the Queen's authority into the fire, where it was burnt to ashes, in the sight of the Queen of Great Britain, not only with impunity, but with some favour and affection evinced by Her Majesty's representative, the Mayor, who appeared pleased and enamoured by Mr Bird's contempt of Her authority, for he countermanded his original order, given for the ends of justice, and permitted John Bird and John Hodkinson, two of the principle conspirators, to remain in court, in this iniquitous and malicious prosecution.

There was then no remedy.

My Lord, and Gentlemen of the Jury! Observe the common *animus* of this prosecution for innocent blood, as well as the blood of the innocent, in the name of the Queen of Great Britain.

What! Cannot Her Majesty, as the Mighty Huntress in her day, before the Lord, go out like the sun, to find beasts of prey enough for her blood-hounds, without hounding them to sacrifice the liberty and the life of an innocent man, upon her criminal altars, with the bloody hands of her Law Priesthood?

What! Does the *equivalent* Queen of Great Britain, the Mistress of the civilised world in her day, fear the light of the sun, living in a drop of dew, and identified in the name of William Price?

Will Her Majesty the Queen, dressed by her officers of state in her white robes, sprinkled with five and a half pounds of my innocent blood, plundered by her Cardiff officers in her name, under the seal of office, on the first day of December, 1852, present herself *again* at the altar of the Lord her God, to partake of the Holy Elements of His Holy Communion before my plundered blood, is ordered to be restored to me out of which this malicious ex-officio prosecution was presented here on the 11th day of March, 1853, in the Small Debts' Court at Cardiff by the conspirators, in the administration of the Law of the Land?

The learned Judge here, addressing Mr Giffard, by counsel for the prosecution, said here is an action brought for seizing the goods of William Millward. William Millward charges Ann Millward and the bailiff with making an illegal distress – how is it important to the cause that this gentleman (Mr Price) interfered?

Mr Giffard – the evidence shows that a piece of paper is handed to Ann Millward; she said she did not know anything about it, and handed it to Dr Price. He says to her sign it, and she does sign it. She also says I wish Dr Price to manage everything for me.

The Judge – How is it material to the issue tried in the County Court? The question was, whether the two persons charged there were liable to damages for taking the plaintiff's goods, and how is it material whether Dr Price interfered or not? You must begin at the County Court and show that this is material. I cannot see that it is material.

Mr Giffard – it was very material to find out whether authority had been given in Miss Millward's presence to go to the house, whereas the bailiff should have gone to the quarry.

The Judge – If she had denied it in the Court it would have been right. I must fix you in the County Court.

Mr Giffard – Anything may be material; it is for the jury to say whether it is or not. I refer your Lordship to the recent case of Phillpots tried very lately; that did not at first sight appear material.

The Judge – It might do for the purpose of shaking the credit of a witness. Suppose he was asked if he wrote to Chester that would be just as important. Here is an action in which the plaintiff complains that his goods were taken to distress for rent, not· pretended to be due for the house from which they were taken. There can be no doubt that was illegal. The question is – who did it? The bailiff did it, and the bailiff and Miss Millward are the parties sued. I cannot imagine how it is material to the question Mr Price saying that he did not authorise the bailiff to make the distress.

Mr Giffard – There is no evidence to show that Ann Millward directed the bailiff where to go.

The Judge – If Dr Price had been the defendant then you would have been right in fixing him.

Mr Giffard – Dr Price said he never gave directions for the bailiff to go, and if he did not tell him how was he to know where to go?

The Judge – Surely the written authority was there.

Mr Giffard – That was only an authority to distrain. There is no place mentioned. Dr Price told him where to go and what to do.

The Judge – You do not produce this gentleman's (Dr Price's) examination in chief.

Mr Giffard – No, My Lord. I believe it was only one question; he was merely asked if he were an attesting witness to the agreement.

The Judge (to Dr Price) – You can address the Jury further if you wish.

My Lord, and Gentlemen of the Jury! These are the facts, the circumstances and connections of events on which this villainous ex-officio prosecution is based, and the extreme questions I have asked, on which their solution depends. I submit them to your serious consideration to be answered by your Verdict.

My blood, my liberty, and my life, are in your custody this day.

Do me justice!

This villainy, conspiracy and malice of my persecutors thirsting for my blood, have sworn me guilty by perjuring themselves.

Truth, justice and common-sense say No! No! There is no foundation for it. Not Guilty!

My fate is sealed by the word of your mouth!

Your will be done on Earth as it is in Heaven!

With that dramatic appeal, one might feel that Dr William Price was on trial for his life and facing the hangman's noose! In the event, the jury took just 20 minutes to return a verdict of "not guilty". The official record of the trial concludes –

'The result was received with enthusiastic cheering from the densely crowded hall, although it was then a quarter past one in the morning. Repeated rounds of applause greeted the defendant which were renewed when he reached the street, and continued some time with unabated ardour.

Chapter 5

Second Exile

During the 1850s, Price fought many legal battles. The law fascinated him. He revelled in the adversarial nature of the court, and with his swift mind and an oratory worthy of a Cicero, he invariably won. In fact, the idea of losing was abhorrent to him, and defeat when it did come was a psychological shock.

In 1860 he decided to build himself a new and larger house in a wooded, hill site near the Pontypridd Rocking Stone.

'It is a wonderful place,' he said to Megan. 'We shall be within the aura of the Druids. There is a magic about the stone that reverberates down through the ages. It calls to me. It knows that I am the one who will revive the old belief.'

Megan was accustomed to these fanciful ramblings about the Druids, and these days took little notice of them, but the idea of a bigger house was attractive.

Work commenced, and two round towers were built to mark the entrance. Those towers are still there, photographed by such modern tourists as may happen to know for what they were intended. But the house was never even begun.

An argument started with the owner of the land, who took out a court order restraining Price from what was alleged to be trespass.

To the amazement and fury of William Price, the case was declared against him and a fine imposed with costs. He flatly refused to pay, whereupon a warrant was issued for his arrest. The following morning, police were outside his house. Megan was out shopping. Iarlles who was then 11 years of age and a bright child, exclaimed, 'Daddy, don't let them get you. Hide inside the trunk.'

The trunk was a huge, old-style cabin-type which could accommodate a man easily enough. Reluctant though he was to indulge in the indignity of hiding from his enemies, Price was even more reluctant to go to prison. He climbed into the trunk and Iarlles slammed down the lid, then went to the door, proclaiming with wide-eyed innocence that 'Daddy isn't in'.

The police made a perfunctory search of the house, but, incredibly, did not bother to look in the big trunk. Perhaps they just did not expect the richly eccentric and dominating personality of Dr Price would be bothered to hide.

Shortly after their departure, Megan returned and went for help. Three friends came that night and carried Price inside the trunk out of the house.

Two days later he was in Paris. It was to be six years again before he was to return to Wales. In that time Megan would have left the house to marry a surgeon in Cardiff.

The Paris that Price found in 1860 was a different place from the city he had left in 1845. George Haussmann, Prefect of the Seine, was half way through his gigantic task of creating the Paris that the 20th century would know. For seven years his armies of diggers, more destructive than any invading horde, had ruthlessly swept away whole streets and courtyards, blazing the grand new boulevards through the old city, so that they radiated like the points of a star from the Arc de Triomphe, the Etoile.

Napoleon 111 was a dreamer who had a vision of a new Rome. 'I. want to be a second Augustus,' he said. 'Because Augustus made Rome a city of marble.' To make his dream a reality, he had conjured up the doer – Haussmann.

The citizens forced to leave the warrens of insanitary and disease-ridden tenements were naturally not happy. Even today, slum-dwellers often prefer to cling to the familiar. But there was another side to that situation. A cartoon in a newspaper showed the figure of Cholera protesting to Haussmann that the destruction of the old dwellings had left him homeless.

The Emperor, during his early years of exile in England, had been much impressed by Hyde Park and London's numerous squares. He determined not only to copy these but to better them. Accordingly, the Bois de Boulogne was taken over by the city and transformed into a great park with two lakes. On the edge of the park the racetrack of Longchamps, intended to be superior to Epsom, home of the Derby. Vincennes was also made into a park with three lakes.

Price went again to see his old friend John Masklyn who was still practising.

'You will find that not a lot has changed here medically,' said John. 'A thousand different theories as to the causes and treatments of disease are flourishing as in Britain. It was confirmed only a few years ago that typhoid is caused by impure water, and I am among those convinced that it is true, but in the country there are thousands still dying of it. Smallpox is rampant still, too. Did you know that as long ago as the seventeen nineties Napoleon Bonaparte ordered smallpox vaccination for everybody? But there is still great resistance to it, especially in country areas.'

'Never mind all that,' said Price. 'I have a living to make. I know not how long I may be here this time. Another six years, perhaps. I have written to Megan to arrange with my bank so that I can receive money to set myself up here.'

He soon found that life in Paris was lived at a much less hectic pace than it would be in London. In England, the railways were spreading their snaky lines like the arteries of the body across the land. The smoky cities sucked in the peasants from the countryside to labour in the 'dark satanic mills'. The Industrial Revolution was in full spate. France was not interested.

In a new publication founded in the year of his arrival and entitled Le Tour du Monde, Price read that 'the best way to make life happy is to make it useful, modest, simple and not too busy. Avoid careers which involve hard work. In France we should not seek to make money with that unflagging zeal which seems to apply in England and in America.'

It was vastly different from the work ethic which applied in England, where labour was now enshrined almost as a religion, enabling Britain to become the workshop of the world.

Nevertheless, the exile from Wales could not but admire the superbly elegant city that he saw arising around him.

Price soon had his plate up again and was receiving patients, Homeopathic tablets came directly to him from the still flourishing Hahenemann laboratories, and it did not take him long to make social contacts. He was now 60 years of age, the same age as the century, but vigorous and looked a lot younger, which he always confidently attributed to his vegetarianism.

He had taken no active interest in politics since his ill-fated Chartist days, but one encounter made him aware that political forces and feelings ran deep behind the facade of polite Parisian society.

Pauline Joubet was a young woman who came to him for treatment for a minor complaint. She seemed to be intelligent and better educated than many females of the time. Learning that he was from Wales, a land of which she had actually heard, she asked if the people of his country were 'likely to rise against the oppressor English as our people of Brittany would like to rise against the French?'

Price was amused. 'I know about Brittany. They speak a language akin to that of the Cymru, and they have similar customs of bards and eisteddfod. Once I suppose we were one, for even Britain takes its name from the land of your Bretons. But as to rising, the English control half the world with their empire.'

'You must not give up hope, Doctor. Unity is everything. One day the workers and the peasants will rise everywhere and triumph over their rulers.'

She left him feeling that here was in some ways a kindred spirit, but an unrealistic one.

He had heard that there were in Paris a number of small, secret, revolutionary societies, numbering probably not more than hundreds, dedicated to some vague ideal of socialism. Masklyn, who knew all about the latest political movements, had mentioned a book entitled *Zur Kritik der Politischen Oekonomie*, published in the previous year by a German agitator called Marx who had now settled in London.

It was some weeks later that Price was aroused in the middle of the night by a heavy knocking on the door of his surgery. Pulling on a cloak, he hastened downstairs to the door. In the dim glow of the lamp that he had picked up, he recognised Pauline Joubet.

'Monsieur le Docteur, I beg of you please to come. A friend of mine is injured. It is not very far from here. He is bleeding badly.'

'Take him to hospital,' said Price, grumpily. 'They will attend to his injuries. It is all they are useful for.'

'Please Monsieur; I beg of you to come. He will not go to hospital. I have told our friends that you are a very brilliant doctor. Better than any at the hospital.'

'That is true, very true.' Price, as usual, never had any modest inhibitions about agreeing with anyone who praised him, especially where medical skills were concerned.

'We can pay,' she urged. 'We have no need of charity.'

'Very well. Wait here while I dress.'

He dressed quickly, seized his emergency bag, and followed the woman through the lamp-lit streets, coming presently to a tenement building in a somewhat disreputable quarter which Haussmann's picks and shovels had not yet reached. Here she led him up narrow creaking stairs to a fourth floor apartment the door of which opened after she had given what sounded like a coded knock. A gaunt, bearded man, who gave Price the impression that, had he been a building he would have been condemned long ago, ushered them inside.

51

On a couch lay the patient. A young male, probably in his mid-twenties; deathly pale, but conscious. He was bare to the waist with a bandage tied clumsily round the left shoulder area. Blood was seeping through it.

'How long has he been like this?' Price asked.

'He had the – accident – some hours ago,' the man replied.

Price carefully untied the bandage and stared at the wound. He had not had much practical experience with this kind of thing. Gunshot wounds were not everyday happenings in rural South Wales, but he knew that a ball fired by pistol or musket was inside the shoulder.

'This man has been shot. Was it a duel?'

'You are a doctor,' said the man. 'What does it matter how it happened?'

'Can you help, please?' said Pauline. 'Can you take the ball out here, without him going to hospital?'

'It will be a lot easier in hospital.'

'He cannot go there. They will ask questions. We do not want questions. Please help us.'

'All right. I will do what I can. Get some boiling water for my instruments, and towels or sheets for the blood.'

He always carried a quantity of chloroform, and under his instructions the patient· was lifted onto a table. Once he was unconscious, and with Pauline passing instruments to him, Price succeeded in extracting the ball.

'Your friend will live,' he said, as he sewed up the wound. 'With care and luck, that is. But he should not be moved for several days.'

'We will have to move him soon,' she replied. 'They may come looking for him.'

Price busied himself putting away his equipment, and did not bother to ask who 'they' might be.

'That is up to you. I have done my best.'

Pauline led him back through the maze of streets to his house. 'I will not bother to ask questions,' he said. 'Obviously the less I know the better. I just hope there will be no repercussions on me for this night's work.'

'You are a foreigner. Do not involve yourself in our problems. One day, when we have built a better world, all the workers and peasants in your country as well as ours will be free.'

Price smiled. 'I have heard such things before, when I was with the Chartists in Wales. But you cannot break the power of the landowners and capitalists with guns. I do not know what you are doing. I do not

52

want to know. But violence does not work. One day we will succeed, but it will take generations.'

'You are a good man, doctor. You should meet our leader. Although he does not approve of violence, either. We are not foolish enough to oppose the system with guns. We have so few. But sometimes the rulers are afraid of us. They think we are stronger than we are. If you would like to meet him, you might find it interesting. I will let you have a letter.'

She left him at his door. He did not expect to hear from her again, but a few days later an envelope was delivered with a note attached. 'Doctor Price, this letter will introduce you to one whose philosophy inspires our movement, Pauline.'

The letter was addressed to a man of whom Price had heard: Pierre Joseph Proudhon, French philosopher of revolutionary bent, known for his advocacy of anarchism.

Well, on his previous visit to Paris he had met and enjoyed conversing with Heine, so why not see what this Proudhon could offer in the way of civilised discussion? He would need to be careful, though. He had no desire to be mixed up in French politics and find himself in trouble with the authorities, even, perhaps, deported. That he certainly did not want.

He found his way a few days later to an address off the rue Madeleine; a respectable district indeed. He struck the imposing brass knocker with his usual forcefulness. The man of the people obviously had a better life-style than most of the common people whose cause he championed. Price recalled having read somewhere that one of Proudhon's most well known sayings was that 'property is theft'.

A maid led him into a book-lined study and took his card and the letter. A few minutes later there appeared a large, shambling figure looking like a Neanderthal man who had been untidily stuffed into a suit with waistcoat and cravat. He had the thick, gnarled fingers of an outdoor worker, which was surprising, for Proudhon had been a printer for much of his life. His eyes had half circles of fatigue, but his voice held a quiet dignity.

'Pauline speaks well of you, Doctor Price. I understand that you were kind enough to render some service to a friend of hers who was in a difficult situation.'

'I merely did what a doctor should,' Price replied. 'I do not know the cause of the man's injuries and did not enquire.'

Proudhon smiled. 'It is best not to. I do not know, either. Some young men are impatient for change, and think they can make a new world over night. They get involved with reckless elements, and our police are sometimes inclined to shoot before asking questions. However, enough of that. You would like to know something of our problems here in France?'

'I am interested in all the conditions of human society. But I am a guest in your country. I may have to stay here for some years and you will appreciate that I cannot afford to get mixed up with agitators. I might be asked to leave.'

'I do understand that. People have called me an anarchist, but that is an exaggeration. It is true, I see the centralised state as an oppressor, but the answer is not a total abolition of law but what I see as a loose federation of communes, or cantons. The tyranny of money should be ended by abolishing it. We should go back to a system of exchange in which goods would be valued by the amount of labour put into their creation. The land must be given back to the peasants, and the landlords stopped from profiteering at the expense of their tenants.'

'I do not think that would work in Britain,' Price commented. 'There the peasants are abandoning their land to work in the factories. That does not seem to be happening on anything like the same scale in France. Here, outside Paris and a few other centres, most people still work and live on the land.'

That meeting was the first of several that Price had with the ageing leader of a new philosophy which had, against the wishes of its promoter, caused some young men to resort to violence in the cause of an idealistic revolution only half thought out by most of them.

The Welshman did not, however, share Proudhon's vision of a society based on social equality which was not, it seemed, to be extended to women. 'Woman's place,' Proudhon declared 'is in the home. They are inferior to men, and in the home the father's power should be unlimited.'

Price disagreed emphatically. 'Marriage is a prison for women. They have to sell themselves in return for their keep because our patriarchal society does not train them in the skills that are necessary to earn their own living, and thus be independent of male support.'

Proudhon shuddered visibly at this horrifying concept. 'If women were allowed to earn their own living in equality with men, it could mean the destruction of the family. Many of them would not want to marry. They would also compete with men for jobs, and that would be a terrible situation.'

'Marriage is not important,' Price told him forcefully. 'Men and women should be free to live together without the blessing of a church. And as for work – before I left Wales I heard of an English woman, Anderson I think her name was, who is even now studying to be a doctor. A school of medicine has agreed to accept her, and I do not doubt she will be the first of many.'

Heretical views such as these, with this strange foreigner's ideas of a future in which men would have to compete in the labour market with a 'monstrous regiment of women', soon made it plain that the two had little in common, and after a few visits, Price ceased to go to the house on the rue Madeleine.

There was one aspect of current thinking in Paris which certainly did find favour with Price; that was the strong tide of anti-clericalism that the Revolution of the previous century had created and which was still strong, at least in the cities, although in the countryside the Church was much more dominant.

By the middle of 1861 his practice was flourishing and profitable. From time to time, letters brought him news of Wales, and he was not greatly disturbed to hear that Megan had departed to make a new life for herself taking Iarlles with her.

In England, Charles Dickens had published a new novel entitled *Great Expectations*. Darwin's *Origin of Species* was exciting fierce debate, Sandringham House had been built as a residence for Queen Victoria, and far away in America civil war raged.

Price had bought himself a new *phaeton*, and one fine Sunday in the summer of that year, he took a ride in the Bois, having observed that, since Haussmann had turned the place into a public park it had become the habit of the fashionable classes to go to the Bois to see and be seen.

The lanes were crowded with vehicles, some being of the one-person type like his own, other opulent carriages, the well-groomed horses controlled by liveried drivers.

As he traversed the side of one of the lakes, he noted a young woman driving alone ahead of him. She was dressed in a flowing yellow gown and the *phaeton* was painted the same colour, a combination obviously designed to attract attention. She pulled in suddenly onto the grass and, as he drew level, he saw that she was sitting bent forward, her head on one hand, the reins clutched loosely in the other. His medical instincts aroused, he stopped his horse ahead of her, turned in his seat and called out, 'Madame, are you well?'

She raised her head, and smoky blue eyes surveyed him under long dark lashes. She was good-looking and aged, he thought, about 30. He considered swiftly three possibilities: she could be *enceinte*, feeling faint through a combination of tight corseting and hot sun, or she could be one of the high class courtezans who often prowled the Bois looking for rich customers.

He dismounted and walked back. 'I am a doctor. If I can be of any assistance . . . ' He plucked his card from his breast pocket and proffered it.

She looked at it with interest, then swiftly took her own card from the silken reticule on the seat beside her. 'Madame Christina de Rougeville.' The address was in a district which he knew was just outside the town of Versailles.

'I thank you, Monsieur for your interest, but I am all right. Merely a little tired from the heat.'

From the brightness of her eyes he deduced that there was little if anything wrong with her, and was fairly certain that the apparent distress had merely been a feminine ploy. Which still left him uncertain as to whether he or someone else was the object of the lady's attentions, but from the fact that she concentrated her gaze upon him, and was not looking at any of the carriages passing by, he was reasonably sure it was himself in whom she was interested. Question – why?

'I was very pleased to hear that, Madame. We are sheltered here by the trees. A few minutes and perhaps you will feel able to proceed.'

'You are a foreigner?' she queried. There was not any doubt about that, with the long pony tail in which he wore his hair, even though he tended to be more fashionably dressed these days in keeping with his professional status. There was also the very heavy accent with which he spoke French.

'I am from Wales, but practising medicine in Paris.'

'Ah, Wales; a part of England, I believe.'

He winced at such geographical and cultural ignorance, but he had encountered it frequently, even from quite learned people.

'Not quite, but you could say that Wales is part of the British Empire and shares the same queen.'

For the next few minutes they indulged in general conversation about the beauty of the park, and how the Prefect of the Seine was changing Paris.

'Monsieur Price, you must come to one of my salons. I will send you an invitation. I like to invite people of many professions and at present I do not have a doctor.'

He replied that he would be very pleased to 'accept your charming invitation', and he stood smoothing his hand over the satiny flanks of his horse, feeling the sun-warmed skin beneath his palm as he watched her drive away. Then he mounted his own vehicle and urged it forward behind her, until she turned out of the park and he went his own way.

A few days later a letter came inviting him to attend a salon at the house of Madame de Rougeville on a Sunday afternoon. The choice of day surprised him. People of this class would be surmised, be leisured and inclined to hold their meetings on weekdays because most of them would not have work to go to. However, it suited a hard-working medical man with a busy surgery.

The château was a large establishment behind high walls in spacious grounds. Several carriages were already there.

His hostess, resplendent in one of the crinoline gowns then fashionable, greeted him. The large room was decorated in blue and gold and dominated by six huge chandeliers. Alabaster figurines graced occasional tables, and collected treasures of an oriental nature gave an exotic flavour.

He was introduced to a number of people and discovered that this was one of Madame's 'scientific' salons. It seemed that she held gatherings to which men of science were invited, and these salons alternated with others for authors, musicians, actors, artists and even politicians.

Price was quickly a centre of interest, especially from the ladies, and he set himself to exert his Welsh charm with his usual gift for conversation.

It was the first of many such salons to which he was invited. He found himself attending both the scientific and the 'mixed' salons. What did surprise him was that Madame – a wealthy widow as he soon discovered – gave him no more personal attention than most of her other guests, but this seemed to be explained on his second visit by an eminent professor who engaged him in conversation.

'You know, Doctor Price, that Madame is a collector – of people, or, rather, of men I should say, since she has little interest in those of her own sex. But her interest in men is purely impersonal. One might use the word platonic. Like many intellectual females she is frigid – cold as the snows of the Polar regions.'

'You consider the lady intellectual?'

'Undoubtedly, the description is more than courtesy. She has written and published a biography of Madame de Pompadour and a history of the Cathar heresy of the Middle Ages.

'There is a story about a musician – not a well known one – who was in love with her. One day the foolish fellow tried to chase her through the gardens but fell and sprained his ankle. She allowed him to stay in her house for several days while he recovered, but it did him little good. He had to spend the afternoons lying on a couch with his ankle bandaged, while Madame played the piano and sang him love songs while wearing – so gossip has it – the most revealing of gowns, a tantalising way to treat a man.'

Price was to have some experience himself of Madame's tantalising ways. A guest at one of the salons that autumn, a writer of some distinction named Bisset, was complaining about his young son who had asthma, and about the doctors who had failed to do anything to relieve the condition. Madame de Rougeville was nearby, and said to Price, 'Do you know of any treatment for asthma, doctor?'

Having imbibed rather well of the wine, he was in an expansive mood, and replied, 'Homeopathy, Madame. I have known some remarkable cures.'

In fact, although Price had been using Hahnemann's little tablets for some years, often with success, he had never actually tried them on asthmatics.

'I have heard of this treatment,' said Madame, plying her Japanese fan thoughtfully. 'Doctor Price, if you come here at two of the clock tomorrow afternoon, I will take you in my carriage to Monsieur Bisset's house to see his son. Bring these famous tablets with you.'

M. Bisset's feeble protest that he would send his own carriage for the doctor was brushed aside. Madame had taken charge.

Price went home thoughtfully. Why had he not kept his mouth shut?

That evening he paid a hurried visit to a Dr Kruger who had taken over the Hahnemann laboratories after the founder's death some time before.

'Asthma?' said Kruger. 'You need nux vomica and a high potency of belladonna. I can supply those, but beware that there are no immediate cures and asthma is not always easy to treat. We do not know the cause and homeopathy takes time to achieve results.'

'I know that,' said Price gloomily. 'This lady and the boy's father will be expecting an instant miracle cure.'

Kruger smiled. 'I think you have boasted too much, my friend. Doctors should beware of seeming to make promises that nature and God may not allow us to keep.'

Price departed with a supply of the tablets and a depressed feeling. He had little faith in God and knew that nature was a capricious mistress.

The following day, leaving the surgery in charge of the assistant whom he was now employing, he made his way to the chateau. Madame was ready with her elegant carriage, its brasswork glittering in the sun and two footmen ready for the journey to M. Bisset's residence about a mile away.

Sitting beside Madame in the carriage, he was much aware of her nearness. She was, undoubtedly a very handsome woman, and in the prime of her appearance. Her hair was piled high today in the current fashion. She would have spent a long time with her hairdresser that morning. very likely dictating letters at the same time.

'Tell me, Doctor Price; when you lived in Wales, were you married?'

'No, Madame; but I have lived with several ladies at various times. I do not intend to allow any church to force me into the confines of formal marriage.'

Since Megan was the only woman with whom he had actually lived, he was, as usual, meandering down one of the minor tributaries of truth, but he could never restrain himself. Sometimes it seemed to him that his exaggerations were probably true.

'Ooh, là là. You are frank, Monsieur, but I like that. In France, we honour the sacredness of marriage but it is the woman who is expected to keep the vows that the Church enforces. The man is free to maintain a mistress – or several. I think perhaps I would like this Wales of yours, where neither men nor women need be tied by the shackles of marriage.'

'You would cause havoc in our society, Madame. You are too beautiful – too much *la grande dame*.'

She raised to her lips the fan which she seemed to carry so often, turned and looked at him over its top, her eyes like deep bright lakes within their lash-fringed shores. He was obviously saying the right things.

'It seems that Wales raises interesting men who know how to pass pretty compliments. You must tell me more – later, when we are at leisure.'

They reached the villa where lived M. Bisset, and Madame descended from the carriage, moving with the grace of a well-fed cat.

The Bissets greeted them. Madame Bisset, a colourless type of woman accustomed to living in her husband's shadow, hovered anxiously like a fly afraid that two carnivorous plants had invaded its domain. Her husband was also suitably deferential.

They were conducted to a room in which a thin, pallid boy of about twelve years sat at a writing desk. 'Jean is doing work set for him by his tutor,' M. Bisset explained. 'The boy attends to his lessons very diligently and the tutor considers that he is exceptionally gifted.'

'Allow me to listen to the boy's chest,' said Price.

The mother unfastened her son's shirt and Price gravely listened to the typical wheezing. Then, folding his stethoscope, he looked around the room, cluttered with furniture and heavy curtains, the closed windows shutting out the bright day. 'Do you always keep the windows closed?'

'Oh, certainly,' M. Bisset hastened to assure him. 'Our regular doctor who comes to bleed him says that we must keep him sheltered from the dangerous miasmas that arise from the fields.'

'Nonsense! There are new ideas in medicine of which your doctor is not aware. It is believed now that patients with chest ailments should not be confined in rooms. They should breathe good fresh air. It is what their lungs need. Open those windows, and let the child go outside as long as the weather is warm. Let the healing sun shine on his skin. And give him these tablets.' He placed the bottle and a piece of paper on the table. 'Follow the instructions exactly, and do not handle the tablets with your fingers.'

'Will he – will he get better?' Madame Bisset asked anxiously.

Price, his ego at stake, plunged in deeply. 'Fear not, Madame. Give your son those tablets – I will see that more are supplied – and he will improve. But you must follow my other advice also. Fresh air, fresh air and sun. And no more bleeding. I do not wish to hear that you have failed to follow my instructions.'

With superb arrogance he swept out of the room. Behind him he heard Madame de Rougeville say, 'He is a marvellous doctor!'

'Will he really be cured?' she asked him in the carriage.

'If I say he will be cured – he will be cured,' Price said.

Her eyes glowed, and he basked in their warmth. But what happened when they arrived back at the chateau was to destroy any illusions he may have had about Madame's 'warmth'.

For our knowledge of the activities of William Price during his second exile in Paris, we have to rely on the correspondence between himself and one who appears to have been among his very few close friends, Cledwyn Hughes of Cardiff. In a letter written just after this episode, Price expressed his feelings bluntly.

'We alighted from the carriage, and the driver took it away. Then Madame fluttered her long eyelashes at me with sufficient vigour to blow the petals off the roses. She turned, gathered up her skirts, and began to run – yes, run, I tell you – across the lawn towards the house. A momentary impulse to run after her assailed me, but I checked it. I did not intend to let my feelings, my desires, overtake my common-sense like some foolhardy Goliath. Damn it! I am sixty years old and a respected man of medicine, not a raw youth chasing a coquettish girl. Also I remembered what I had been told about the incident between this woman and one of her admirers, how the man had sprained his ankle and been sung at for days. That would not happen to me.

'I sauntered in her wake as befitted a Welsh gentleman in full control of himself and aware of his dignity and status. When I entered the house, she was not visible in the hall, but a few notes on a piano guided me into the music room where Madame was seated at the instrument, some of the glow having left her eyes as she beheld me stroll in.'

'You did not run after me,' she said, in a voice which indicated haughtiness mixed with a measure of irritation.

'Oh, God, I thought. The woman wants to sing to me! She is probably offended because I was ungentlemanly enough not to sprain my ankle running after her.

'Madame,' I replied, 'I am not accustomed to running – unless it be to catch a train, and even then I expect it to wait for me.'

'Be seated,' she commanded. I sat on one of those cabriole-legged chairs dating from the period of one of their kings – Louis 15 or 16, I don't know which, and she began to play and sing, in a fairly passable voice, although it would never take her to the Paris Opera. It was one of those tedious love songs that seem to go on forever. And I very soon began to get bored, and thought longingly of how much more melodious – and more in tune – were Welsh male voice choirs.

My physical desire for this woman had ebbed like a fast-receding tide. I realised that her charm was of the surface kind that would wash off in a shower of rain. Beneath the tightly-laced dress, the rouged cheeks, the high tower of her hair, there was only a hollow, a nothingness. She was a cook who lays a table for a man, sumptuous meal is proffered, but when he takes his seat at the table – the dishes dissolve.

She stopped in the middle of her second song, and I was suddenly and guiltily aware that my eyes had momentarily closed.'

'You were going to sleep!' her voice rose . . . 'You were going to sleep – how dare you when I am singing? Monsieur, I ask you, I demand, how dare you sleep while I sing to you?'

I rose and walked slowly over to the piano. 'Madame,' I said, and I placed one hand on top of her own as it lay on the piano keys. She snatched the appendage away as if I had bitten her. That fellow was right. The woman was frigid. Even her skin felt cold.

'In my country,' I said, 'men are not accustomed to being played with. We *make* love, we do not waste time singing about it.'

She stood up, her face flushed redder than the rouge. 'Go from my house. You insult me. GO!'

Her voice had risen to a scream, as she flung out a dismissive hand pointing to the door as if in some stage melodrama. I bowed, and said, 'Perhaps that would be advisable.' Then I walked, with dignity and measured tread, out to my carriage.

'That, I do assure you, was the end of my brief flirtation with the world of the Paris salon. I was not particularly discomposed. The gatherings had been becoming somewhat tedious. I had, however, made a number of acquaintances that would be useful socially. I had also acquired several wealthy patients who could afford to meet my more exorbitant bills.'

In the following weeks, Price paid regular visits to his patient at the Bisset household, taking with him fresh supplies of the homeopathic tablets – and presenting his bill.

To his great relief, the boy showed clear signs of improvement. The parents had kept to the fresh air and sun regime, despite the protestations of their regular doctor, a more orthodox practitioner. At that time, in France, there was no medical ethic against one doctor moving in on another's patient, no matter how much the first doctor might dislike it.

'You are lucky,' Kruger told him when Price mentioned the improvement. 'Asthma is a difficult situation with which to deal. The causes appear to be many. Sometimes the treatment works, sometimes not.'

Price was practising in Paris in a decade when medicine was undergoing a dramatic change, emerging from old ways into what might be described as the more 'scientific' mode. Methods such as bleeding and purging, which must have killed more patients than they saved, were being seriously questioned. In 1824, Byron, suffering from a fever at Missolonghi, was purged and bled for several days by a team of doctors. His last words were 'the doctors have murdered me!'

In the 1860s, Pasteur was working in Paris, Lister was Professor of Clinical Surgery at the University of Edinburgh; Simpson, inventor of chloroform, had published a book on acupressure. All of these pioneers were, of course, to endure their share of derision and obstruction by the orthodox medical establishment, an attitude still existing today, with homeopathy and herbalism outside the pale, and most medics still refusing to believe that 'we are what we eat'. William Price was well ahead of his time, having abandoned bleeding and purging long ago, if indeed he had ever used such methods, and being among the first to introduce homeopathy to Wales. Later, having read Simpson's work, he was to make use of acupressure.

Life continued uneventfully for some months, and then Pauline Joubet came back into his life – with unfortunate results.

She appeared one day at his surgery with a complaint so minor that he wondered if it was merely an excuse to get to see him.

'Doctor Price, I am going to a lecture tomorrow night by one of our comrades from Germany. He will be talking about how we should prepare for the revolution that must one day come. Will you accompany me to the lecture, please? You will find it interesting, and there are so many things I would like to talk with you about.'

She smiled at him across the desk, and for the first time he saw how good looking she really was. He liked the way she brushed long slim fingers through her blonde wavy hair in a slightly nervous gesture. She moved well, too. As she entered the room he had noted the sway of her hips.

As he wrote later to Cledwyn Hughes, 'I had no great desire to sit through a lecture by some political firebrand, but suddenly, sitting in my surgery, looking at this attractive young woman who wanted my company, I realised that I had had little feminine companionship for a while, so I agreed to go with her. I was to regret the impulse.'

He certainly was.

The lecture hall was a dingy place, and Price was not impressed by the audience. Mostly young, the kind of politically active youth that was to be found in any capital city. A lot of them obviously from the Sorbonne. The speaker was a German refugee with a tale of repression in his home country. There was probably more symbolism in what was said than Price was aware of, for the Franco-Prussian war, when Paris would be besieged, was only a few years in the future. But this night, Price realised how far away was his own youth. Back in his Chartist days he would have revelled in all this rhetoric about overthrowing the oppressor class and introducing a republic. Then he had been saying much the same things himself. Now he was sixty-two, a respectable man of medicine running a prosperous practice. Youth was an alien race.

Politely, he joined in the applause at the end. They made their way out. 'You will come back with me?' she said.

'Where do you live?'

'It is not far from here. I have my own apartment. I have been left my home now for two years.'

He began to be interested. It turned out that she lived in one of the new blocks on one of the equally new boulevards. She had left home shortly after completing a university course. He gathered there had been disagreement with her parents who were very middle-class and detested the revolutionary crowd with which she had become involved. A familiar story of youth in revolt against bourgeois values.

But in Wales or England, no young woman of good family would be likely to be living alone in an apartment. She would certainly have some kind of chaperone with her.

She made him coffee and they sat on the divan. The apartment was spacious and well furnished. He gathered that her parents paid the rent. The walls were hung with a number of paintings, all her own work. Art had been her subject and it seemed that she even sold a few, the money going to 'the cause'.

Presently, she went out of the room, returning shortly wearing a very flimsy night garment. It was obvious that she had nothing on underneath, and he could see through the almost transparent material the pink tips of her breasts.

He stood up, surprised. He hadn't expected . . .

She held out a hand, and took his. 'We shall go to bed,' she said.

Price was later to write to Cledwyn Hughes. 'I will tell you I was astonished. But, remembering Yvonne, the daughter of Captain Phelps with whom I had an amorous encounter during my first residence in Paris, perhaps I should not have been so.'

In the bedroom, eyes glowing with animal pleasure, she threw away any final shreds of inhibition and begged him to possess her now. As her arms closed round his neck, his body was suddenly aflame. He divested himself of his clothing faster than he had ever done, and as he did so she flung off her single garment.

He could feel her wanting coming off her in waves, and fire spread through him as he brought his stomach against hers. Her hair, loose around her creamy shoulders, was scented webbing against his already sweating chest.

Then they were on the bed, and he cupped her breasts in his hands, sucking at one sensitive peak and then the other. His hand caressed along her body, down over the curving belly and down into the soft delta of Aphrodite between her thighs.

'Now!' she gasped. 'Now!'

He was on top, pressing into her, and at the summit of their ecstasy, she cried out for him to press her harder.

He was to write to Cledwyn, 'Throughout that night we made love as if we were members of some species facing imminent extinction.'

They parted late in the morning with exhortations to meet again soon, although the exhortations were more from Pauline than from Price for, in the brittle dawn light over the rooftops of Paris, a cloak of protective instinct was beginning to fold around him. He was delayed opening the surgery, and could have used some hours of sleep which he had not had.

The next day, he decided he would take Pauline out to dinner, hoping that the woman was not going to be too possessive.

He wrote a letter of invitation to dine with him at the Cafe Anglais on the Boulevard des Italiens. This establishment had been opened some years earlier and had become a favourite eating place with Price. He took the letter to her apartment after surgery and, finding no response to his knock, pushed it through the letterbox. A note of gushing acceptance reached him by a messenger later. He frowned over her reply. It assured him of her undying love. That he found disquieting.

The dinner passed off reasonably well. They dined on *culotte de boeuf salomon* with *potatoes Anna*. Although the Cafe Anglais was a popular place with the bourgeois of the Second Empire, he knew that it was also patronised by Proudhon, so he assumed that it would not entirely offend her political susceptibilities. She looked round and commented caustically upon some examples at adjoining tables of what she referred to as 'social parasites', but nevertheless seemed to enjoy the food and the attention.

As they left and walked out into the night, she dropped the cannonball on his head. 'These places are nice to go to occasionally, but we must not make the habit of frequenting them when we are married.'

They were entering the side street in which he had left his cabriolet along with the carriages of other diners in the care of the watchman. Keeping a tight hold on himself, despite the mounting alarm and the icicles that were clattering up his spine at her fateful words, he handed the watchman a few sous and helped Pauline into her seat. He drove out of the street and turned towards her apartment.

'Listen,' he said through gritted teeth. 'There is no question of marriage. I do not believe in that outmoded institution. Do not think of it.'

She drew in a deep breath that must have seriously strained her corseting, then she exploded; her voice tearing through the clatter of hooves and wheels on the street. She used French words that he had never heard of but which he suspected were decidedly not ones that a lady should use.

He pulled on the reins. 'Get out!'

She hit him across the face, and it stung, as one of her rings cut his cheek. She jumped out, and was shouting after him as he drove away. It was a light summer evening and only just dusk. People were staring, and he hoped fervently that none of his patients were on the street.

He helped himself to a large cognac when he reached the security of his room above the surgery. Bitch! Termagant! Politically fanatic and looking on a doctor as a good catch. Would she take it further? She could cause of lot of trouble if she decided to pursue him.

He soon found out that she could and did.

Letters were delivered: vitriolic, threatening, accusing him of having used her selfishly and betrayed her; one even mentioned the possibility of charging him with rape, which alarmed Price considerably. In another she was contemplating suicide and would leave letters to 'my poor father and mother' explaining that he had driven her to do it. Price was uncertain which course would be the worse for him. Of the two he might survive the suicide more easily, even though it would damage him professionally. He began to hope that she would commit suicide and put an end to the persecution.

He wrote to Cledwyn: 'I am in despair with this fanatical woman. She says I abused her, took advantage of her innocence. That is a grotesque accusation. The woman was no virgin and seduced me. I do assure, you, my friend, it was most decidedly not the other way about. But when a woman makes this kind of accusation, so often the victim that is mere man is not believed. It is easy for her to portray herself as the wronged and innocent maiden because I am twice her age. Being a foreigner will not help my cause either.'

He began to fear the knock on the door, believing it might be the police, that she had made charges against him. He had visions of a trial, prison, and the deportation, to face prison again back in Wales. Then, suddenly, the persecutions ceased. Days passed and nothing happened. Had she killed herself? Was her body lying in her apartment, yet to be discovered?

The revelation – and the relief – came on the tenth day of the silence. He was driving along the boulevard when he saw her. Alive – walking arm in arm with a young man and *laughing*!

He nearly boiled over with rage, but was thankful that she did not see him. At least she had apparently found a new distraction and perhaps would forget him. This was evidently so, for he heard no more of Pauline Joubet and was able to sleep soundly.

Not long after this happening, he was returning home late one night on foot, having been called out to attend a patient who lived not far away. His surgery and living quarters occupied the first two floors of one of the older apartment blocks in a side street off one of the boulevards.

Sitting on the pavement, backs against the wall, were two figures, male and female. They were only yards from his door and he had to pass them to get to it. Impulsively, he stopped. Thousands of down-and-outs littered the pavements of Paris as of any other capital city. That was (and still is) nothing new. Normally he ignored them. One had to do so. They were some of the casualties in the eternal battle that was daily life in a free capitalist society. He had had enough to say on that point when he used to rail about the poor of rural Wales and those on the streets of Cardiff.

But tonight he was undergoing one of his mood swings, and suddenly felt compassion. 'Do you have nowhere to go?'

'Would we be here if we had?' the man replied, not unreasonably.

Price looked at him and made a sudden decision. 'Come inside. I will give you food.'

In the gas light of his living room he could inspect them clearly. The girl was probably in her late teens. Slim to the point of thinness, fairly good looking and would have been better still with some feeding. The man was older, perhaps early forties. Unshaven, somewhat hollow-eyed and a bit sunken in the cheeks. Both had obviously been on the streets for some time.

They wolfed down the coffee and sandwiches that he gave them, and sat warming before the stove.

'How do you come to be homeless?'

The girl answered first. 'My father left us, then my mother took another man, but I did not like him. He – troubled me, so I left. I met Andre on the streets. Now we are together. We want to stay with each other.' She touched the man's hand, and smiled at him.

'I was married,' he said, sipping his coffee and staring at the stove. 'Too young. We had two children. But we quarrelled – often. Like I said, we were too young. She had a lover. I left. I've heard since of my eldest son. Grown up now. He is a priest. Would you believe it? My son a priest! Of course, I have not seen him for years. It is so long I have been on the road, all over France.'

'Do you know where your son is?'

The man's face twisted into a bitter smile. 'No, I never will.'

Shortly afterwards, Andre went into the room in which Price had installed one of the new water closets, and the girl leaned forward, lowering her voice. 'I think I know where his son preaches. It is the church of St Cecilia on Montmartre. I know because I go into churches sometimes and I have seen the name of the priest at St Cecilia. It is Frossat, the same as Andre's. Of course, it may be coincidence, but I like to think not. It would be nice if the priest could know where his father is, so that perhaps he might help us.'

Price, too, lowered his voice conspiratorially. 'Bring Andre here tomorrow night. Tell him that I will have supper for you both. I will see if I can find this son.'

He let them sleep that night in his living room, giving the girl a blanket and a pillow for the divan and Andre a blanket to sleep in the big armchair, although he suspected they spent most of the night on the divan in each other's arms. There was just enough width for two – very close. Once he awoke in the night and heard the girl's soft laughter. He envied them. They were young – well, she was – and in love. Yet they had nothing but each other.

They departed after breakfast. It was Saturday and he did not have a surgery in the afternoon, so he went up the hill of Montmartre, where he easily found the church of St Cecilia amongst the turning windmills.

He went inside. A thin scattering of worshippers knelt in the pews. Two elderly women were lighting candles. He was in luck, a priest was just emerging from a door by the side of the altar. He was certainly young enough to be Andre's son. Price stopped in front of him. 'Could I speak with you, father?'

The priest was instantly attentive, attracted by Price's foreign accent and his pony tail. 'Can I help you?'

'Your name is Frossat. Do you have a father named Andre, whom you have not seen for many years?'

The priest was startled. He led Price into the small room where priests changed their vestments, and listened as his visitor told him of Andre and the girl.

'Obviously from what you say, this man will be my father. I would like to help, maybe I could find him a job, somewhere for them both to live. If he will accept help.'

'I don't know if he will. He has some pride, but he also wants to take care of the girl who is with him. It is possible that for her sake he will let you help. If you would like to come – they will be with me tonight.'

'I will be there. It is good of you to take this trouble for strangers. Are you of the faith?'

Price hastened to deny that he was 'of the faith'.

'I have no faith. The trappings of your church mean nothing to me. I do not accept your god or the folk tales of primitive tribes that make up your Bible.'

Father Frossat looked amused rather than indignant. 'Yet you are doing good to strangers. Perhaps the meaning of Christianity has touched your heart without you knowing it.'

Price did not intend to waste his time arguing with a mere priest, and a Roman one at that. 'Even pagans can do good,' he said. 'I will see you tonight.'

That night, as his two visitors sat eating the supper that he had prepared for them, there was a knock on the door. He opened it and let in Father Frossat. 'Andre,' he said. 'I think you two should talk with each other. I will leave you for a while.'

Andre stood up, with an astonished expression. Plainly he guessed immediately at the identity of the visitor. Price went hastily into his kitchen and remained there hoping that Andre would not indignantly walk out. But he had guessed rightly. Concern for the girl if not for himself must have triumphed. After a while they called him back, and there was high drama and emotion between the three.

'I am taking my father and this young lady back to my church,' said Father Frossat. 'I can accommodate them for the night and tomorrow we will see how to help them.'

Andre clutched at Price's hand. 'Had I known what you were doing I would not have come here tonight. But now, I am glad I did. Perhaps it was intended that you should find us.'

The girl put her arms round Price's neck, and kissed him. Her warmth and the sweetness of her gratitude touched him, and when they had all gone out into the night he felt, unusually for him, suddenly old. But the feeling did not last. A glass of champagne, his nightly tipple, soon restored the Price ego and he was ready to battle with the world again on the following day.

Shortly after this incident, Price, seeking an outlet for his oratory and opinions, joined a debating society, and in a letter to Cledwyn he included some extracts from a lecture he gave on the subject of 'How Odd is Your God'.

'I told them,' he wrote in the letter, 'that Voltaire said if God did not exist, man would have had to invent Him. And that is what we have done. This deity in which Christians, Jews and Moslems all believe is a necessary fantasy, born out of early man's need to see some pattern in an unknowable universe, to feel the security of a father figure watching over and guiding us. Of course since this God is all loving – a concept that clashes with the injunction to 'fear God' there has to be some explanation for the existence of evil. So the Devil was invented. But even this clashes with the concept of an omnipotent God, since, if your God is omnipotent then He would not allow His puppets on earth to use their free will in the choice of evil deeds.

'Yet, I do believe that there has to be intelligence of some kind behind this strange and wonderful universe. And it may be that we are all part of that cosmic intelligence, that the difference between a human being and a piece of iron is that we are animated by a spark of that intelligence, what some might call a soul But I find the concept of individual immortality very improbable. When a drop of rain is falling from a cloud towards the ocean, it is an individual entity, but immediately it hits the ocean it loses that individuality and becomes one with the whole.'

Price concluded the letter by mentioning that half the audience applauded him with enthusiasm, the other half appeared to be offended, which seemed to be how life generally treated William Price. And he loved it that way.

In the spring of 1862 an odd little incident occurred. Price had made himself known to the managements of several of the large hotels which catered for foreign visitors. Sometimes, when a visitor was taken ill, the hotel would have to send for a doctor, and it was useful to have one handy who could speak the language of the guest. Price was therefore on call to deal with English-speaking guests. Hotels in the 1860s were not equipped with multi-lingual staff.

One day he was summoned to an hotel where an under-manager conducted him to a spacious suite on the fourth floor. 'They are Americans,' he explained. 'Wealthy. The daughter appears to be ill.'

The door was opened by a tall man wearing a fashionable matching braid-edged frock coat with waistcoat, check trousers and cravat. 'You the doctor? Speak English?'

'I am and I do.'

'Fine. I'm George T. Rafferty from Georgia. I never met so many folks around here that don't speak English. I'm over on a business trip, brought my daughter Susy with me because she speaks French, learned it at the posh college I sent her to. But she wasn't well coming over on the boat, and today she takes this funny turn. Come and have a look at her.'

He led Price into one of the bedrooms where a good-looking young woman of probably about 20 years lay in bed, looking pale. A black maid stood by.

'I don't want none of that bleeding,' said the father. 'We don't hold with it much these days in the States.'

'Do not worry,' Price told him. 'I don't, either.' He proceeded to examine the girl with his stethoscope, looked at her eyes and tongue, took her temperature.

'You carry on,' said the father, 'I got some papers to attend to. Come and tell me what you think when you've finished.'

He went out of the room, and Price sat looking at the patient. She looked back at him with wide blue eyes that were, he felt, a little too innocent, 'How do you feel?' he asked. 'I can find nothing wrong with you.'

The girl hesitated, cast a look at the black maid, and said in a slow southern drawl. 'Doctor, I gotta tell you there's nothing wrong with me.

But please don't tell my father that.'

'I have to respect a patient's confidence,' he assured her. 'But I will also have to tell your father something, so you had better confide in me and I will see what I can do.'

'We're from New Orleans, the south. My father is here to buy guns for the Confederate army. His partner, Ned Zigler, came with us. He wants to marry me. Pop likes the idea, too. I don't. I figured if I seem to be ailing all the time, Ned will cool off. He's a very fit guy, gets impatient with folks who are always being ill. So I want him to think I'm sickly, too weak to give him the sons he wants.'

The maid interrupted, twisting her hands nervously and looking at the door. 'Mr Zigler sure is an impatient gentleman; always wantin' to be up and doin' things. Never sits still.'

Price was, for a moment, baffled. 'This is a desperate idea. It will not be easy to maintain when you do go home. Your father will become alarmed at your condition and will want other doctors to see you. They will either discover that there is nothing wrong, or will decide that you have all kinds of obscure diseases and will start treating you with medicines that will give you real ailments.' Knowing the members of his profession, Price was fairly certain that the latter result would ensue. The unfortunate girl would become a medical wreck if she had to keep up the pretence for long.

'Mr Zigler may abandon his desire to marry me. That is my hope.'

'Miss Rafferty sure will decline if she has to marry that Zigler,' said the maid.

The absent Mr Zigler was obviously unpopular. Price felt he would like to help the girl, but in the long term she was clearly on her own with her problem. 'Listen, I will tell your father that the sea journey has exhausted you, and I will have a harmless medicine made up and sent in. That is the best I can do.'

She gasped with conspiratorial delight, his words serving to raise the barometer of her spirits by quite a few degrees.

'That would be marvellous, doctor! Are you French?'

'No, I am from Wales.'

'My father is from Ireland. He knows people in Wales, and I have seen it on a map.'

Price's heart warmed to this southern belle. She had seen Wales on a map! One stage better than never having heard of it.

'I will wish you good luck,' he said. 'More than that I cannot do for you.'

He went out into the main room of the suite where Mr Rafferty was pouring over papers on a table. 'Well, what's wrong with the girl?'

'I judge that the long sea voyage had debilitated your daughter, leaving her very weak. She was probably not strong to begin with.'

'Humph! She's always been strong enough at home. She rides and ain't been ill much.'

'Well, I will have a medicine sent in later. Instructions will be on the bottle.'

He sent a messenger later with a bottle of a harmless concoction, and heard no more of the Raffertys, but often wondered if Susan managed to avoid marriage with the so odious Mr Zigler.

A new experience came the way of William Price when, in the spring of 1864, he received a letter from M. Bisset informing him that the gentleman would 'like to call on Dr Price next Saturday on a matter of Social discourse'.

From the phrase 'social discourse', Price deduced that his visitor was letting him know that the impending visit had nothing to do with the health of his son who was, at Price's last visit, progressing well.

When M. Bisset arrived he hastened to assure his host that his son was indeed well. 'In the past, Dr Price, Madame Bisset and myself have come to look upon you as more than a doctor, rather also as a friend, and we are wondering if you might care to join us, along with little Henri, in a holiday which we are planning to take. You are doubtless aware that the south coast of France, where the people grow oranges and lemons, and the sun shines for much of the year, is now very much more accessible. A railway service was begun last year from Paris to the town of Cannes. A new hotel has been opened there called the Grand, and it is to that town that we propose to journey and stay for three weeks. We would appreciate very much your kindness in accompanying us at our expense.'

Price quickly grasped that what M. Bisset wanted was his presence in case little Henri should be taken ill, and the Bissets were offering a free holiday in lieu of medical fees. Normally, Price would have rejected such an offer, but the winter in Paris had been a long one and he was feeling jaded. The idea of three weeks in southern sun was attractive. He could leave the practice in the hands of the very capable assistant that he was then employing. So he agreed.

The coast that was later to be known as the Riviera was already attracting a growing number of upper class English visitors who were spending winters there, despite the rigours of a long coach journey ending on precipitous mountain tracks. The coming of the railway had already made a vast difference, with hotels now being built at Cannes, Nice and

Mentone, mainly for the English sun-seekers.

The attractions of the Azure Coast had been further publicised by *Letters from Cannes and Nice*, a book written by Margaret Brewster, daughter of an eminent Scottish physician, and appearing in print to describe her stay during the winter of 1856-7.

Not that Margaret Brewster was entirely enamoured of the region. She wrote that 'The native female servants are stupid, idle and ignorant and far from cleanly. They demand excessively high wages and expect free wine and coffee, and they have an aggravating habit of shaking hands with their employer. One lady was so agitated by the constant shaking of hands expected by her cook and other domestics, that she was obliged to put a stop to it.'

Another English visitor was Augustus Hare who wrote *A Winter in Mentone* describing a stay there in the winter of 1860-61. He appears to have spent some time trying to find a restaurant that suited his very English taste, but eventually he discovered one 'from whence we got a dinner which was tolerable, after it had been stripped of its oil and garlic, and had some extra cooking bestowed upon it by our own servants'.

Hare did mention how polite the natives were to strangers, and described how a servant, on hearing that the English were very fond of fresh green grass, went up into the mountains and brought back two pots full of grass as a gift.

The Bissets had decided to go at the end of April, although they agreed that this was somewhat late in the year, but at least they would be back in Paris before the 'great heat of the southern summer'. No one, not even the English, relished the idea of actually spending summer on the coast. It was essentially a place for winter residence.

The four of them left Paris at 11 a.m., accompanied by Henri's tutor and Madame Bisset's maid. They arrived in Cannes late the following evening and it was a tiring journey. The idea of sleeping and dining cars still lay some years in the future. On this early rail link to the south, travellers slept in their seats and took their own food, or bought from the vendors at stations.

The Grand Hotel, however, when finally reached, lived up to its name and was a welcome oasis of comfort after such a journey. The night air was warm and seductive with strange Mediterranean scents. The air also held something else, less attractive, as Price found out when he went to bed – and awoke some time later to the thin whine of mosquitoes. It would be a long time yet before this major drawback to life on the azure coast could be tackled by science.

The Bissets, as he discovered in the following days, were great walkers. They liked to hire a diligence and go out into the mountains to walk. They visited Grasse, which had been a centre of the perfume industry since the 16th century. They went to Mentone which they found to be well occupied by English residents and renowned for its lemon groves.

Price later wrote at length to his friend in Cardiff about his holiday on the Mediterranean with the Bissets: 'An amusing family. M. Bisset is a pompous little man but harmless with a moderate sense of humour. His wife has as much colour to her character as a rain-washed street in Llantrisant on a winter's day. All the views she expresses – when she ventures to express any – are such as have previously been conveyed to her by the not very scintillating mind of her husband. Little Henri is unlikely ever to cause his parents any trouble. He obeys every smallest order given to him because he lacks the necessary independence of spirit to do anything else. The maid is a simpleton and the tutor a little man in every sense of the word, over-awed by his surroundings and as cravenly deferential.

'Unlikely companionship for me, you will be thinking, and of course you are right. However, I was feeling much jaded at the end of a long winter, and the prospect of three weeks of a free holiday at a 'Grand' hotel in southern sunshine held considerable appeal. Although my companions have been, at times, irksome, I would exercise the utmost tact, patience and forbearance to such an extent that our relationship remained amiable throughout. I was amused by the revelation that my hosts liked to play croquet, this being a game at which I have had some experience. There are two courses at Cannes on which we played frequently during the first week, less so during the second when the enthusiasm for the game appeared to decline with the Bissets. Possibly this could have been because I usually won!

'I found Cannes to be a pleasant town, and likely to become a sizeable resort at its present rate of growth, especially on account of the increasing number of English who settle here for the winter. Indeed I have become so accustomed to hearing only French during the past four years that I find the English language almost grates upon me, and I heard much of it on the coast. I did encounter at the Grand a family from Tredegar, but, sadly, they were that type of Welsh people who had not bothered to learn the language of the Druids. They spoke only the tongue of the Anglo Saxon. I treated them politely but distantly.

'There appears to be little poverty down here, certainly nothing resembling the conditions of misery which apply in many of our cities in Britain. Most of the local people seem to have their little plot for the growing of lemons or olives, and of course they do not require the same expenditure on clothing and fuel for winter warmth. On several days I have indulged in sea bathing, the action of salt water on the skin being very efficacious. I persuaded the Bissets to let me take little Henri into the water with me. The sea is actually warm here, like a tepid bath. The Bissets themselves could not be led into the water.

'The markets are well supplied, and Nice wine, mixed with water, makes an agreeable beverage. I have also become fond of fresh anchovies fried in olive oil. The local water melons, too, are delicious. The light here is bright and all colours more brilliant than in our softer northern climes. Green grass, though, is in short supply due to the low rainfall. The men play boules on parched earth. The life pursued by English settlers here seems to be most colonial. I believe that many of them feel as if they are residing in some far corner of Empire and that the simple French peasants are their subjects, ignoring the fact that these 'subjects' are white of skin, which is surely unusual.

'Before making this journey, I took the trouble to read a book by one Tibia Smollett. Entitled *Travels Through France and Italy*, this describes the author's experiences on the south coast of France in 1763, although at that time Mentone and Nice belonged to Italy. Smollett appears to have shared the normal English attitude to foreign food. He 'abominated' garlic and took with him large stocks of chocolate, tea and larks' tongues. The English did not like to live off the country and I have to say that they appear to have changed little since Smollett's day.

'I found Monaco to be a pleasant little place, ruled almost as a little kingdom on its own by the Grimaldi family. The town has an English lending library and there is also another foreign element here. I was told that, since the coming of the railway, members of the Russian nobility are now staying for the winter in Nice and Cannes. I judge that, as an area in which to escape the rigours of northern winters, this region will become increasingly popular.

'The journey back to Paris was tiresome, and I feel that it would be enterprising of the railway company if they were to include special carriages with couches on which passengers could sleep. One might then arrive at one's destination more refreshed than is the present case. Surely also it should not be beyond the reach of human cleverness for food to be served to travellers on such lengthy journeys.

'It is spring in Paris, and very welcome is the sight of the daffodils trying on their sun-bonnets in the parks. I return to work and to my patients much refreshed. My assistant has looked after everything very well.'

It was shortly after returning from the coast that Price had to attend the funeral of a wealthy businessman who had been a patient of his and with whom he had been friendly. He sat through the church service, repressing his own cynical thoughts when the officiating priest said that 'God in his infinite wisdom has chosen to take our beloved brother at the age of thirty five'. At least one member of the congregation would have liked to stand up and say: 'I ask why? Where is the wisdom in leaving a widow and four children?' But then, he had had many similar impious thoughts when sitting in chapels back in Wales, listening to the preachers rambling on about a god who was all loving and yet whose wrath one should fear.

After the service, he stood with the other mourners at the graveside, and looked round at the great amount of space taken up by the cemetery. He wrote to Cledwyn:

'More than ever I note the folly of taking up land from the living by burying bodies in it. Dust to dust, they say, and these preachers would have us believe that the body is only an empty shell, the soul having gone to a better place, so they say. Why, then, let the vacated shell occupy precious land? Let the cleansing fire reduce those shells to ashes. When I come home I would like to start a campaign for human cremation. That would set the chapels aflame!'

It was to be many years yet, however, before his dramatic act that was to make human cremation possible in Britain.

In another letter to Cledwyn about this time, he mentioned the lowly status of women in the Second Republic, although it was little different from that prevailing in Britain.

'They place women on a pedestal in many ways,' he wrote, 'but repress them at the same time. A woman can be sent to prison for two years for adultery while the man goes free for the same thing. Indeed, if a husband kills his wife for adultery he is not guilty of murder, but his wife would merit the severest penalty for killing a brutal or adulterous husband. A wife cannot sell property without her husband's permission, and if he dies his widow is allowed to keep the children but should she remarry she has to obtain the permission of the late husband's nearest relatives as to whether she may continue having care of her children. Rousseau, along with Proudhon of whom I wrote to you long ago, approved of these conditions.'

Several times during 1865 and 1866, various people sought to persuade him to invest in such enterprises as a nursing home for the rich elderly, a private hospital, or even to join in the funding of some dubious project for medical research. Paris was alive with medical quacks advancing the most outlandish theories for which they needed only money. But, as the end of his exile drew nearer, Price determined to hang on to his capital so that he could return to Llantrisant with enough to buy a practice and a house.

He wrote to Cledwyn: 'The medical profession here has a great deal of political power. Out of a National assembly of 231 members, 33 are doctors. Most powerful of all medical men is Dr Philippe Ricord, personal physician to the Emperor. His treatise on venereal disease is accepted as the gospel by everyone, and his mansion in the rue de Tournon contains five fabulous salons for his patients. One is for the common folk, one for women, one for friends, one for patients with special recommendations and the fifth for other doctors. Sculptures and paintings by such as Van Dyke and Rubens are said to adorn the walls. I doubt that this man's rate of cure is any greater than mine.

'You would be astonished at the range of cures offered by doctors. More than half of them appear to have published books advocating the weirdest of treatments. A Dr Leuret, author of a book called *The Moral Treatment of Madness*, ties his patients to planks of wood and douses them with cold water. A Dr Piorry, author of *Commonsense medicine*, claims to cure many ailments by deep breathing and spitting. A Dr Giradeau is known to bribe newspaper editors to publish articles praising his treatments, although many of those so-called treatments are in my opinion rubbish – and dangerous rubbish.'

Chapter 6

The English Woman

William Price returned to Wales in June, 1866. It was the year that Henry Irving made his debut on the London stage. H.G. Wells and Ramsey MacDonald were born. Dr Barnardo opened his first home for destitute children, and Elizabeth Garrett-Anderson had graduated as the first woman doctor in Britain.

Many things had changed while Price had been away. Fashions, for example. He read in an issue of *Punch* that 'The crinoline at length is going out, thank goodness! but long trailing dresses are coming in, thank badness! In matters of costume lovely woman rarely ceases to make herself a nuisance; and the length of her skirt is now almost as annoying as, a while ago, its width was. Everywhere you walk, your footsteps are impeded by the ladies, who, in Pope's phrase, 'drag their slow length along' the pathway just in front of you. Sad enemies to progress they are in their long dresses, and a Reform Bill should be passed to make them hold their tails up.'

Punch, side-stepping the small point that it was mostly men who designed and dictated female fashions, was, as usual, sarcastic at the expense of women.

It did not take Price long to buy himself a practice at Llantrisant and to establish himself in an oddly-shaped house which he named Tŷ'r Clettwr. Soon he was back in the familiar routine. There were more railways now, but to some extent this had made rural communities in areas such as South Wales more isolated because the coach services had declined, unable to compete with trains. This greater isolation was to continue until the motor car began to arrive in the 1880s.

Adjusting himself to the lilt of the Welsh tongue after six years of French, to countryside after the bustle and hurry of the boulevards, to faggots and laver bread after the variety of French foods, all took some time.

What he also found lacking was intelligent conversation. In Paris he had known and talked with men of letters, philosophers, artists, writers, and even met men of his own profession with whom he had been able to hold conversations on an intellectual level, but there was little rapport between himself and the staid outlooks of local country medics here, many of whom, anyway, remembered what he had said about them in the past.

In addition, he lacked feminine companionship. There are hints in his letters during his second exile, of affairs with more than one woman, but they are hints only. We have no records, and he kept no diaries. That he was sexually active throughout the whole of his long life is evidenced by the scurrilous poems that were written about his philanderings, though most of these were published after his death.

How, and exactly when, he became acquainted with the Englishwoman Vanessa Lawrence we do not know, he never seems to have mentioned her to Cledwyn Hughes, but what has survived is the correspondence between them. It is fortunate for biographers that people in the past wrote letters. Future historians are not going to have an easy time with our own age. Folks whose mode of communication is the telephone, the fax and the Internet will leave no records of passionate entanglements.

What we do know is that their first formal meeting was when he attended a medical conference in Cardiff in the summer of 1868. She had accompanied her husband, Dr C.E. Lawrence, an eminent London physician.

Was there some mutual attraction 'across a crowded room' that led to one of them attempting a closer acquaintance after that first formal introduction? In those days, when ladies of good class were rarely unchaperoned, it cannot have been easy to initiate contacts and arrange clandestine meetings, but of course, there were always ways for the determined.

Although the beginnings of the affair are hidden from us, it seems that shortly after Cardiff, Price went to London for a few days and they met secretly at a time when the husband was away. They had already corresponded using her sister's house in the capital as an accommodation address so that Dr Lawrence would not query any letters arriving at their home.

The sister appears to have inherited Price's letters to Vanessa after the latter's death, and then, perhaps for some sentimental reason – or maybe a feeling for posterity – somehow acquired Vanessa's letters from Gwenllian, the woman with whom Price was living at the time of his own death in 1893, and whom we shall meet later.

The correspondence reveals what seems to have been the only true love of Price's life, for he does not appear to have been a man who could feel deeply about others. For Vanessa, the flamboyant Welshman was total contrast to the placid respectability of her English doctor husband.

The first letter on top of the collection is plainly not the first to be written, whatever preceded it must have been lost or destroyed.

July 2, 1868
Tŷ'r Clettwr.

Dear Vanessa,
But that is a common, English address. I must begin with F'anwylyd. That means beloved. I will remember for ever those nights in South Kensington that we filled with paradise. My probing fingers left marks on your tender skin, I remember. I felt the fabric of my being torn apart in that strange, wondrous rhythm as we merged with each other in the night. You were Aphrodite, immortal Helen for whom Troy burned. I was a leaf in your flame and, yet, I absorbed the fire, and was a god to your goddess. I remember – until the very stars in heaven are cold.

If you deem my words extravagant – that is how I am. I belong to the Druidic dynasty. The magic of the Old Ones runs in my veins. They directed me to you. It was not by chance that we met that evening when the very stars sang to your coming. You entered that trivial hotel robed in gold. The latest fashion, so I hear. Complete with that great feathered hat that made you look like an empress. Our eyes met across that room, and I knew that you were mine and I was yours. What did it matter that you were married? Marriage is a triviality that must not be allowed to stand in the path of a love so grand as ours. Love's incense swirled through that room and raised fires within us, enabling us to snap the bonds of conventional morality. I had to know the sweet wine of your lips, the heat of your body, the glory of your soul.

What did you think of me? But, of course, you told me later. You saw this strange member of the ancient Celtic race and felt that we were destined. You wanted to know more. It was fate that I had already met your husband, otherwise the dull formality of introduction might have been difficult to arrange. But he, little man, did not know what he was doing when he said, so formally 'this is my wife'.

How could he know, how could anyone but the gods on high

Olympus, or maybe the spirits of the old Druids, know that two souls had come together, that a flame had been lit that would brighten the sky and illuminate posterity with our love. You smile, you wonder – who, what is this man who dips his pen into the wine of the muse? I will tell you: I am a poet, as are all we of the ancient race of Cymru, born of a thousand eisteddfodau since the dawn of time. Your praises I can never cease to sing. In this life we are but on loan to each other. Tell me, assure me, that we can enjoy each other while the loan lasts.'

June 14, 1868
(no address was ever given on her letters)

My dearest, most extraordinary, most lovable Welshman.

Your precious envelope I obtained from my sister's residence and took a walk into St James's Park. There I sat on a bench by the water and opened it. I do not have the fine words as you do, with which to express my joy, my delight, to know that you feel so deeply about me. As indeed, I do about you. I sit here wishing that you were with me, and I live again those nights we shared in that hotel room. No bridal bed ever has known the ecstasy I felt in your arms. I still tingle to the memory of your hands caressing my body, of the thrill of your possessing me, so different from the clumsy attentions of my husband, a man whose emotions are in a permanent ice age. He knows little of the needs of a woman. But you, my Druid lover, you do not just *use* a woman, you seem to know my needs. You make love so that I share your pleasure.

I had thought not to sign this letter, for I blush to think that other eyes might perchance to read it. Please, I beg, burn this missive when you have perused it. Do not let such intimacies fall under uncomprehending – and censorious – eyes as could happen even if kept under lock and key. However, sign it I must and do.

With all my deepest love and until our next wonderful meeting.

Vanessa.

There was a gap in the letters for two months, although it is not certain whether in that period there might have been several that have been lost. What we know about Vanessa is that she was then about 30 years of age, had been married to Dr Lawrence for five years. There were no children. She came of a reasonably well off family and it seems had money of her own. A Llantrisant source described her as tall, blonde and

81

very good looking.

August 28, 1868
Tŷ'r Clettwr

My Sweet Vanessa,
You are the lost loveliness that all men seek in their dreams but few
find in reality. The loveliness that tangles at the core of desire and
haunts the ragged edges of a man's sleep. If I could be with you
permanently. If it were possible for us to live together, to see you
every day, to lie with you every night, to hear daily your voice which
is like the lining of a summer cloud, hear your laughter that is a
caress, then would I stand upon a peak of happiness such as mere
mortal man can rarely hope to scale.
Would this be possible? Could we be together? How can you go on
living a life of emptiness with a man who does not recognise your
worth? Would you come to me? Dare I ask you to share the life of a
country doctor? I do dare! Vanessa – leave him and come to me. Tell
me that you will I await your answer.

Reading letters like this, of such poetic fantasy, many women, if
already leading lives which they evidently considered to be very dull,
would be likely to fall for temptation. Here was a man who could weave
dreams with words, and who, with his odd style of dress, his ponytail, his
dynamic personality, must have impressed women. There was disparity
in the couple's ages, Price being 68 but looking, from contemporary
accounts, still a good ten years less and having the vigour and energy of a
man much younger. Vanessa proved to be not immune. She fell for that
strange Celtic charm.

September 8, 1868
Sweetheart

In response to your dear letter, let me quote my favourite poet,
Elizabeth Barrett Browning:
  'How do I love thee? Let me count the ways,
  I love thee to the depth and breadth and height
  My soul can reach, when feeling out of sight,
  For the Ends of Being and Ideal Grace.
  I love thee to the level of every day's
  Most quiet need, by sun and candle light.'

My love for you is deep and, perhaps, beyond reason. But perhaps all true love is so. Empires have been lost for love. Anthony and Cleopatra lost the Roman Empire, Lancelot and Guinevere destroyed a kingdom. It matters not that one was fact and the other fiction. But *we* have no empires to lose. I have but a boring marriage which I can well do without. You are lonely, and a bright soul such as yours should not dwell alone.

You flatter me with your words that ring so fine I think they must be writing them down in heaven. It is difficult to believe that you belong to the same practical and prosaic profession as my husband. You have a spirit that transcends the body. Yours is the soul of the true poet. If we were to be together, as you suggest. If I should come to you, would the reality of daily contact disappoint you? How could I, a mere mortal woman, live up to your poetic image of me? I am the 'Lost loveliness?' Indeed it is lost that I am, lost for want of decision. Should I burn my boats like Cortez? Fly to my lover and let the devil take the consequences? What matters the opinion of a sanctimonious society when two people truly love? And yet – that sanctimonious society is a powerful entity. Everyone would be censorious of us. We would have to live together without the requirement of marriage, 'in sin' in fact. Although, despite society, I cannot count it a sin when committed in the name of love. What to do? My lover, I do not know. I am in despair. My sister, in whom I confide in order to facilitate the arrangement of our correspondence, counsels caution. And there is no one else I dare trust with such a secret. My sister, of course, does not know you – alas.'

In his next letter, Price sought to push her over the emotional brink, to make the leap into his world, to make her lose herself in the magic of his dreams.

Tŷ'r Clettwr
September 14, 1868

Dear Heart of My World,
I have tried to put aside my own desperate need for you my beloved one and to think only for you. More than once you have confessed to me that your life with your husband is an empty and hollow sham, that you have, and indeed never did, have, anything in common, that he neglects you, that you were pressurised to marry at an early age by both your families. This kind of life will destroy

you, and I seem to be the only one – the fated one – to save you. I can do this only by offering you my home and my heart. I will come to London and meet you at the usual place at noon on Wednesday next. I hope that the gods will be kind to us both and that you will be able to be there.

Where the 'usual place' was we do not know, but the next and final letter in the collection shows that he had talked to good effect.

September 28, 1868

Darling,
It is done! All arrangements have been made. Many of my clothes have been taken to my sister's house. *He* is absent at the conference in Paris. I can collect the remainder of my possessions later. I will be on the train which arrives in Cardiff at 2 pm on Monday next. My boats are truly set aflame! I hope to see your dear face on the platform – welcoming me to Wales and to your world.

And so Vanessa came to Tŷ'r Clettwr. What the betrayed Dr Lawrence did about it, if anything, there is no record. But perhaps he felt it beneath his dignity to try to get her back, or maybe he was glad to see her go. We don't know. But it was quite a local sensation when Dr Price's new mistress took up residence in Llantrisant, though by that time the village was accustomed to the doctor's unconventional ways.

Megan had at least been one of them, but Vanessa, southern English middle-class, did not easily fit in. It was in those days a very Welsh speaking area, and Vanessa made no attempt to learn the language. She had studied French at a 'college for young gentle ladies', French being the traditional language of the cultured classes, but she found so much difficulty in wrapping her delicate English tongue around the strange words of the Cymraeg, with its juxtaposition of letters that did not make 'proper' sounds, that she soon abandoned any preliminary attempt that she did make. This did not make her popular, and sometimes caused problems when she went shopping, some of the local shopkeepers seemed wilfully unable to understand the requirements of a woman living in sin who spoke an alien language.

A maid was now employed at Tŷ'r Clettwr as well as the housekeeper, so Vanessa soon got into the habit of sending the maid to shop for food. When clothes were needed she went to Cardiff where there was no language problem in the more upper class shops.

Price was undoubtedly obsessed with this woman, so different from any of his previous amours who had been Welsh and French. His experience of English women had been virtually nil. Maybe it was the difference that attracted him. Also it seems that Vanessa did have some intellectual ability. Like most young women of her class she had been brought up to have nothing much else to do but read the classics along with modern literature, and play the piano. She had also studied something of the philosophers and was able to discuss the works of such as Kant, Schiller, Schopenhauer; she could even talk about Socrates and Plato, having at one stage had a tutor who had provided a classical background to her education.

This obviously enhanced her appeal to Price in addition to her physical charms, and certainly put her above the standard of the long departed Megan.

However, you can't live on Kant and Socrates, nor on sex, either. Acting as his receptionist in the surgery, and doing his paperwork, undoubtedly kept Vanessa busy, providing a new stimulus for her. It must have partly made up for the inadequacy of social life in Llantrisant, at least for a while. Price had a small circle of friends, but they all usually spoke Welsh with each other. In fact, many older people had only a poor command of English.

There must, however, have been conflict between Price's unorthodox and eccentric views and way of life, and the much more staid and respectable background of his mistress.

The wider social life of Llantrisant was barred to her, partly because of the language barrier, partly by the resentment of the natives towards this 'foreigner' with her expensive and fashionable clothes and her patrician attitude towards those whom she was unable to regard as other than rather lowly peasants.

Towards the end of 1869 he took her to the Pontypridd Rocking Stone, that place which had become as sacred to him as any sanctified wayside shrine to a Christian. Here she watched him array himself in his Druidic robes and address to the stone a long poem that he had composed in his own version of Old Welsh.

Price wrote later to Cledwyn Hughes: 'Vanessa does not seem able to understand my affiliation to Druidic beliefs, and openly expresses scepticism when I tell her that I am the direct descendant of a high priest of three thousand years ago and that I am destined to bring back the old faith to our land. She asks how do I know this, and when I tell her that it was revealed to me through my translation of the Stone of the Bards in the Louvre, she says that I must have been having some kind of hallucination.'

Vanessa could not know that all this was part of Price's slowly developing schizophrenia, but she may well have become aware that there was something odd about this aspect of his behaviour, which contrasted so sharply with his practical ability in daily life as a doctor. The realisation that his talk of being a Druidic descendant was not just romantic fantasising but that he really believed it must have come as a shock.

She would never join him in his walks in the countryside. Vanessa preferred to ride. Once they took a holiday at Lyme Regis, and happened upon a deserted cove where he wanted her to join him in naked sea bathing. Vanessa sat sedately under a parasol while he frolicked in the surf.

It could not last. That their alliance endured for two years was remarkable enough. She was a woman of the city, having always lived in London, and Llantrisant was much too small. The people were also, as she would have said 'too small'. She left him in June, 1870, and the preserved correspondence contains a final letter from London.

> Dearest,
> I have very much enjoyed our two years together, and would not have you think that I am unappreciative of the kindness and the attentions that you have bestowed upon me. I do see now, however, that, although truly we have many things in common, there were also factors which divided us. I am not unaware of my own failings, and would not have you think that I am blaming the failure of our love all upon yourself. But I cannot enter into your world of the Druids, and feel that your apparently firm beliefs in this do constitute an element of fantasy. Your peculiar activities at the Rocking Stone I found deeply disturbing. Also, as you know, I did not find the people of your village as friendly as they might have been.
> The memory of our love and our two lovely years together will always burn brightly in my heart. I wish you well and trust that the God in whom you do not believe will guide and protect you.

Where she went we do not know, but Price never saw Vanessa Lawrence again.

He missed her. Oh, yes, he missed the love of his life, the great romance that was to have sent them both soaring to the stars. But not for long. In the December of that year Gwenllian came. The woman for whom there was no grand passion but who was to be with him for the rest of his life, sharing in one of the most spectacular episodes of a long career.

He wrote to Cledwyn: 'I have met the most astonishing lady. She is good looking, charming, thirty years of age and well educated. She is Welsh, I am pleased to tell you, from the north, from a village called Clawddnewydd near the town of Rhuthun, and speaks our language as well as ourselves for she is of the true race. Her father is in some business in the north, of what kind I know not. She had an unhappy marriage from which she fled last year, coming to stay with an aunt in Cwmbran and taking a position as a schoolmistress. She is much taken with me and has agreed to share my house. I have told her of my destiny as the chosen of the Druids and, unlike Vanessa, she understands and says that I have a great future. She is a woman for the years.'

Chapter 7

Coal Strike and After

On the 1st of June, 1871, the coal miners of Aberdare and Rhondda came out on strike for a 5% increase in wages. By the end of the first week 10,920 men were listed as being out, with 3,778 remaining at work.

The pits supplied steam coal, the major purchasers of which were the region's ironworks, and the Amalgamated Association of Miners, comparatively new to South Wales, had hopes that the workers in the iron works would support them. The funds of the Union were inadequate to the upkeep of all those on strike, but, reckoning that, by Union rules, men who had only been in the Union for less than three months were not eligible for strike pay, they could manage to provide 10 shillings per week for each man plus 1 shilling per dependent child.

William Price immediately supported the cause of the miners, and loosed off a diatribe in the local press against the coal owners:

'You are the Welsh Pharaohs who think you can suck the life-blood of the colliers for ever. You have grown fat and prosperous; you own the big houses; you wear the finest clothes; your children are healthy and happy; yet you do not work. Let me tell you. You have been stealing the balance of the low wages which you have been paying them. Take heed, you men whose bodies and souls are bloated by the life-blood of the poor, take heed before it is too late. Remember that the oppression of the Pharaohs of Egypt did not last for ever, and neither will the oppression of the blood-sucking Pharaohs of Wales.'

This expression of forthright opinion brought an invitation from the Aberdare branch of the Union for Price to go and address a meeting of the striking miners, to which he readily agreed.

In a book published in the following year entitled *The Colliers' Strike in South Wales*, the author, A. Dalziel, wrote:

'It occasioned no surprise when, on the 7th of June (one week after the strike had commenced) the Executive of the Amalgamated Association met at the Rainbow Hotel, Manchester, and unanimously passed the following resolution –
'This Executive having fully considered the dispute relative to wages in South Wales, expresses its approval of settling the same by arbitration, as recommended by the Editor of the *Western Mail*, and resolves that a deputation be appointed to go to recommend that the dispute be settled by such means.'

Probably the officers of the Union were impelled to make this offer of arbitration by the fact that such a mode of settlement had already been adopted successfully in the Midland counties; that there existed in Northumberland and Durham, a Board of Conciliation, and that the organisation of such a Board in South Wales would have the effect of consolidating the Union.

On June 9, a meeting was held on the Aberaman Mountain when a Mr Halliday addressed a gathering of the workmen, and prevailed upon them to propose arbitration to the masters.

Price arrived in Aberdare and found accommodation at an inn. That evening, in a packed local hall, he addressed the miners who were pathetically eager to listen to any man of education and learning who supported their cause.

He looked at their faces, many etched with thin lines that seemed as if they were of dust from the seams of coal laid down millions of years ago in the earth, waiting for men such as these, slaves of their time, to grub in the darkness at the behest of their masters.

The chairman, a shop steward named Arwel Roberts, introduced him: 'Doctor William Price, a son of Wales who fought in his youth for the Chartists of years ago, and was exiled to foreign parts for his pains. Tonight he comes to support our cause.'

Price rose at the table on the platform to the applause.

'Men of the valleys. In this age of progress when men of science and learning tell us that they can make a better world for us all, when our engineers build railways and bridges and tunnels, and ships driven by steam, when the homes of those able to afford it can be lit by gas instead of candles. When we saw, twenty years ago, the Great Exhibition in the Crystal Palace, we rejoiced in that display of the arts and culture and industry of the British Empire. Yet, in this age, you men of the valleys are as much slaves as were those of ancient

Rome, lashed to the galleys of their ships, as much slaves as the black people who once worked in the cotton plantations of America before President Lincoln, freed them from their shackles. The Negroid race walks in freedom, and Rome is gone with the dust of centuries. But here, in our land where the Druids once walked, where our ancestors survived the invasion of the legions and kept alive the songs of the bards, the sweet music of the harp, the glory of our poets. Here is still slavery. The masters who drive you live in their big houses, waited upon by servants. They pay you a pittance and live on the profits from your labour. Your task, down in the dark hades of the earth, is not only arduous, it is also dangerous. Most of you know of comrades who died down there in the blackness because the masters heeded not your safety. Why should they, when they know there are plenty of men desperate to earn even a pittance, eager to take the place of those who die?

'It is a disgrace, nay, a sin, even, that women should have to slave alongside you in such appalling conditions, and children, too, in some mines. Long ago, at the urging of the noble Lord Wilberforce, Britain abolished the slavery of the black people and used the Royal navy, at great economic inconvenience to the nation, to stamp out that evil trade on the high seas. That was an act greatly to the credit of the nation and our empire. Why, then, having freed the Negro, do we still have slavery in our own land and of our own people? The rich masters have their big houses and acres of land. Such property, when earned by the sweat of men, women and children in the depths of the earth is theft (Price cared not that at that moment he was virtually quoting Proudhon with whom he had so often disagreed). You are asking only for an extra five per cent on your already miserly wage, and that at least must be granted, or heaven will surely take revenge on those who deny it to you. Not even in a factory where the most intensive methods of securing output are employed do we find workers driven to the same limits of physical endurance as you are driven in the mines.'

His listeners were not learned enough to know that with that last sentence he was quoting from a report written by Frederick Engles thirty years before, and that Engles had been writing chiefly about conditions in the mines of Lancashire.

The audience stood and loudly applauded him. Many crowded round to give 'the famous doctor' a handshake.

As they drifted out into the night, Arwel Roberts said, 'Doctor Price, would you care to come with me tomorrow and visit the family of one of our members, see for yourself how we live? Then perhaps you can tell people the truth, for it does not get told. The newspapers are owned by the mine owners. They print what they are told to print, and it is not in our favour.'

Price agreed to meet the chairman next morning, and retired to his room at the inn to write a quick letter to Gwenllian in which he told her that 'My heart bled to see these men, tired and old at thirty five from the appalling life they lead. They were pathetically grateful to have my support, little though it be of any practical value to their cause.'

When Arwel conducted him the next morning to a street of dwellings where the miners lived, Price was pleasantly surprised to find them of somewhat better quality than he had expected. They had been built by the colliery owners because, when coal had been first mined here, there had been no habitations within easy distance, so accommodation was essential to attract a labour force to what was a fairly desolate valley.

In the kitchen-cum-living room there was a coal-fired cooking range with a back boiler to provide hot water, for all the village had piped water, which many others in the mining valleys of the region certainly did not. There was a sink with draining board, lighting was by oil lamps. In those parts in 1871 gas was available only in the towns and then usually in the better class of homes.

The house to which Arwel led him was occupied by one Owen Evans, miner, and his wife, Gwen, and five children. Gwen looked to be in the mid-thirties, but Price knew that she was more likely in the early twenties, old and worn out with the harshness of the life plus five children and two that had died when young.

'We've only got the Union pay,' said Evans. 'I reckon we'd starve without that. Meri here,' he pointed to the eldest child aged 10, 'she worked down the pit for six months, helping load the wagons. Some of the women were down there, and one girl, up the street here, had her baby there. With my wage and what she got, we just scraped along. I don't know what will happen to us if the strike goes on for long.'

Price looked round the home. A zinc bath hung on a nail on a wall. There was a carpet – with holes in it. The clothes of all were patched and worn. Outside, he understood, was an earth pivy.

'Would you leave here if you could?' Price asked.

'Cutting coal is all I know. There is no work antwhere else and, anyway, where would we live?'

An unanswerable question. 'What are the conditions like down there?' he asked.

'You get used to it,' the man replied. 'We have to work in narrow seams. Mostly we are naked, so hot it is you know. The women are naked to the waist, they and the children fill the wagons and pull them to the shaft where it is hauled up to the surface, but we needed the money. They masters must be made to give us more.'

Price, brimming with anger at such conditions, gave the man all the cash that he had with him, and walked away with Arwel Roberts.

'The masters,' he said, 'are worse than the aristos of old used to be with their serfs. There were many in those days who did care for their serfs and were not badly disposed in their treatment of them, but now we have a new breed of men, a lot of them English but, sadly, some also of our own kind. They care nothing but for the profit they make from a man's labour, and every extra penny has to be dragged out of them.'

'We have to win,' said Arwel, 'but you can see that this is a time of much suffering. It has been difficult enough to build up a union, many are still afraid to join, and it is possible that the masters will try to bring in labour from outside to replace us. There are plenty of men who are desperate for money, and willing they will be to help break the strike.'

Arwel was right in his prediction. A. Dalziel describes in his book how the miners did indeed recruit strike breakers, many being unemployed colliers themselves. Dalziel wrote:

'Although it was the desire of the masters that the men should bring their wives into the area, not more than six or seven women accompanied the strangers. At so early a stage, the men said that they would prefer waiting to see how the employment suited.

'Notwithstanding the good intentions of the old hands to keep the peace, crowds of men and women lined the railway and station at Mountain Ash, to greet the strangers with hisses and groans. Mr Halliday and Mr Macdonald were on the spot to enjoin them to be orderly. No more hostile demonstrations, however, took place, and during the sojourn of strangers in the district, the only disturbances caused were by the wives of the old colliers, but they, despite the bravado evinced at the outset of their engagement, these professional strike-breakers soon lost heart. On entering the villages where the masters had arranged accommodation, they invariably received the cold shoulder. The shopkeepers to a man refused to serve them with a single article, and even the masters themselves had difficulty in the immediate neighbourhood in being supplied with any goods intended for strangers. If any of them had mining skill, which is to be doubted, the excitement and exceptional state of affairs rendered them utterly unfit to do that amount of work which they might at home have been fairly competent to perform.'

Price was subsequently interviewed by one of the local newspapers and expressed his usual forthright condemnation of the masters, but not a word was printed. One of the coal owners was a major shareholder in the company that ran the press in that area.

After 12 weeks the strike was settled with the usual compromise. The men went back to work for a concession of 2½% instead of the 5% originally demanded. Both sides were, inevitably, the losers, although the owners could stand the loss of profits much better than could the miners, who took a long time even to recover what they had lost.

Back in Llantrisant, Price was despondent for a while at his failure to do any good for the down-trodden and the oppressed. He railed to Gwenllian about the inhumanity of the owners, the evil of the system which allowed the minority to live in their big houses and exploit the many.

'I think of those girls who have to go down the mine, while the daughters of the owners are brought up in the soft life, learning how to sew and embroider and play the piano in their drawing rooms, bored because their lives are empty and useless – except to be married off and breed useless daughters and wastrel sons. The politicians in London boast of our great empire, and the Queen is Empress of India, but the very coolies in the fields, the blacks who cut the sugar cane on the plantations in the Indies, they are better off than women and children who toil in the dark earth. That man Wilberforce abolished slavery. A fine and good thing many people said, but he should have paid attention to the slavery of his own kind as well.'

Gwenllian tried to soothe him. 'You have tried. It is not your fault that you failed. You are not young anymore, and there are people here, your patients, who need you. For them, at least, you can do good.'

'Aye, you are right, woman, as always. But failure hurts. Perhaps, in the Chartist days, I should have encouraged that fellow Jones to seize Newport. Perhaps we should all have risen, like the people did in France, nearly a hundred years ago.'

'What good did it do the French?' she countered. 'There was bloodshed and killing and then the wars, and in the end they brought back the king. You cannot fight the world. Do what you can here in the way that you can. That way you can leave some good behind you.'

He held her hand. 'Woman, you have more sense in you than any man I have known. Of course you are right. I talk too much, I dream impossible dreams too much. I am not Saint George able to slay dragons.'

He fumed some more, especially about the church and the preachers who did nothing to support the miners, but finally simmered down. She brought him his glass of champagne, and then it was time for surgery. He was back in the routine, helping people in the way he knew best, which was, as he acknowledged in a later and calmer state, better than leading revolutions that only ended in blood.

Besides the increasing use of homeopathy, he was now well into acupressure. He had even taken on a nurse – Florence Nightingale having made nursing a respectable profession – and trained her in the skill of pressing the right nerve centres for the appropriate complaint.

In 1872 there came to his surgery a new patient, John Roberts, who had recently come to live in the vicinity from Anglesey. One day, Roberts said, 'Doctor Price, have you ever heard of the Anglesey bone-setters?'

'No, indeed, Mr Roberts. I have not. But you are going to tell me. How do they 'set' bones?'

'There are several men practised in the art. They can cure many ailments by what they call manipulating the bones to set them right when they go wrong. It began with a shipwreck, way back in the seventeen thirties.'

'Shipwreck?'

'It was a Spanish ship, broke on the rocks in a storm. A boy was rescued and brought up by a Welsh family. It turned out that he had the gift of bonesetting from his people in Spain where it is a well known art. He began by mending the ailments and injuries of animals on the farms, and then he began treating humans. Now, one of his descendants runs a flourishing practice in Liverpool.'

The story intrigued Price, always keen to investigate new and unorthodox methods. He made further enquiries, and discovered that a bone-setter was still operating in Anglesey, a man named Evan Davies at Ty'n Llan Farm, Bodedern. Becoming interested, he went to Bodedern in the summer of that year, and was intrigued to watch Evan Davies at work on a stream of patients. Price did not know it, but he was watching the birth of the science of orthopaedics. Ty'n Llan is still occupied today, and a plaque on a wall commemorates that here was born Hugh Owen Thomas, father of orthopaedics.

The visit to Ty'n Llan aroused Price's interest, so much so that he later made the effort of journeying to Liverpool and meeting Hugh Owen Thomas personally at his surgery, number 11 Nelson Street, a house since destroyed during an air raid in 1941.

The two men must have been an interesting sight when they met. Price wore his tartan tunic. His pony tail was now quite long and he had taken to growing a beard. Thomas presented an equally arresting figure. Of medium height, he had a dark moustache and pointed beard, thick-lensed spectacles and a black seaman's type cap pulled down piratically over one eye. He always dressed in a black frock coat buttoned up to the neck. Unlike Price, he was a chain-smoker.

The two appear to have got on very well, and corresponded afterwards until Thomas' untimely death from pneumonia in 1891. Price was one of the first to be shown in Thomas' workshop the Bed Knee Splint which he had designed and made himself. This invention was to find its greatest use in army hospitals during the first world war.

Despite his new-found enthusiasm for bone-setting, Price did not go so far as to try to practice the technique himself. For one reason he was probably far too busy to devote the time to what would have had to be an intensive study. He did, however, send certain of his patients who had had accidents to see Thomas in Liverpool.

In 1875 there occurred an interesting encounter Price did not bother with going to medical conferences except very rarely, and then usually no further than Cardiff, but it seems that in this year there was some kind of medical event being held in London which he did decide to attend. One day, he appears to have been having a drink in a Soho pub, by arrangement, with his old friend Cledwyn Hughes, with whom he had corresponded so lengthily during his second Paris exile.

What Cledwyn did for a living, and where he lived at this time we do not know. There is no record of him in the Price story other than as a correspondent, except for this one meeting. Cledwyn, possibly seeking to find some diversion for his friend before he returned to Llantrisant, said, 'You have always been interested in politics, especially the revolutionary kind. How would you like to meet a man who claims to have invented an entirely new economic philosophy which he claims will change everyone's lives?'

'The only man I can think of who fits that description is the German writer, Karl Marx.'

'Oh,' Cledwyn was disappointed. 'You know him?'

'Not personally. I read his *Das Kapital*, or what purports to be the first volume of an incredibly long opus. It was published a few years ago.'

'Would you like to meet him? He used to live in Dean Street but has moved to another part of the district. I have met him on several occasions. I could introduce you. A peculiar personality does not seem very happy with his relations and fears that he will be dust before the revolution can come about.'

The revolutionary fervour of his early years had long faded in Price, and the brief stirrings that he had felt during the miners' strike were four years behind him. He had, with the passing years and some degree of prosperity, suffered the inevitable fate of ageing rebels. He had become conservative with at least a small c.

Curiosity, however, impelled him to agree to meet the creator of the theory of surplus value and prophet of class war.

He was lingering on in London after the conference because he wanted to visit the British Museum to which he had not been for many years. So, on the following afternoon, Cledwyn led him to a street which was home to some of the poorest of foreign refugees and immigrants. Here, Marx lived, in a permanent state of disagreement with his family, a condition which had not been helped by the revelation that he had fathered a child by Helen Dulmuth, the maid who had been with the family for forty years.

Some days later, having returned to Llantrisant, Price wrote to Cledwyn thanking him for his efforts and hospitality.

I found your friend, Marx, a fascinating personality, not the least on account of his coal-black hair matching those equally black and piercing eyes. Judging from the condition of the apartment I gather that he is less than well off. Indeed that only remittances from his friend Engles in Manchester have maintained him for many years.

We spent, as you will recall, several hours, not so much discussing with your friend as listening to the passionate exposition of his dialectical materialism theories, and his firm belief that one day the workers and peasants will rise up. Years ago, when an ardent Chartist, I would have agreed with him. Now, being a gentleman of mature years and what I like to think is a mature philosophy. I am perhaps more in tune with reality, with human nature as it is than Mr Marx, who seems to me to take a rather naive view of humanity with his continual use of that phrase 'historical inevitability'. He admitted that he had been confident of revolution in Germany in 1848 and could not understand why it had not happened. He told us that revolution must occur where there is an educated industrial proletariat. That seems to leave out Wales. In short, I was less than impressed. These armchair prophets can make it all sound credible, but I remain unconvinced by men who seem to live only for their dreams. The new order may look fine on paper after an afternoon in the library, but human nature in its infinite diversity and irrationality foils many fine plans which have only cold logic to support them.'

About this time there is related one of the many stories (maybe apocryphal) of Price's activities. True or not, it is a story typical of him and worth believing. A local butcher came to his door one day and said, 'May I ask your advice, sir? If a dog entered some premises and stole a leg of lamb, what action would you suggest?'

'I would demand that the owner of the dog pay for the meat,' said Price.

'It was your own dog, sir!'

'Indeed it was? How much was the lamb worth?'

'Five shillings, sir.'

'Well, here is your five shillings.'

As the pleased butcher turned away, Price called him back. 'You owe me six shillings and eight pence.'

'What for?'

'Legal advice!' said the doctor.

Chapter 8

Shock! Horror!

On January 10, 1884, the 5-month-old Iesu Grist died. The child had ailed from birth, though Price had firmly proclaimed that this was the son whose destiny was to restore the rule of the Druids to the ancient land of Cymru, as had been foretold in the inscription on the stone in the Louvre which he claimed to have deciphered. Now, despite all his medical skills, the prophecy appeared to have failed.

'I was wrong.' He pulled the edge of the blanket over the small, still face in the cot. Candles flickered up towards the oak beams of the low-ceilinged bedroom in the house of Tŷ'r Clettwr on the hill outside Llantrisant. A coal fire burned in the tiny grate. For 18 days since the child's last illness began it had never gone out. 'It was a misinterpretation of the message in the stone.' His face lightened. 'Perhaps you will have another son and he will be the one.'

The prospect of breeding another who might be the druidic messiah seemed to arouse little enthusiasm in the grieving mother. Gwenllian brushed away the cloud of black hair that hung in disorder to her shoulders, uncared for in these last days and sleepless nights of tending her doomed son. 'Hair as dark as the night that lies between the stars,' he had called her crowning glory. But she had no concern for appearance at that moment.

'You are an old fool, William.' She dabbed at her eyes with an already sodden handkerchief. 'He was an ordinary boy, but he was mine and he is gone. I should care for your druids. They are gone, too, and will not come again. No more will my little Iesu.'

He laid a gentle hand on hers as they stood by the cot. They had made an odd couple since the day she had moved into Tŷ'r Clettwr. The doctor, as old as the century, but tall and straight and rugged, lined of face and long of beard; and the willowy Gwenllian, at 28 taller than most girls of the region with her casual yet elegant handsomeness, the full lips speaking of both sensuousness and refinement. The black skirt and white blouse that she wore today showed off her figure when most decent Christian females preferred to hide their contours lest men had their imaginations aroused.

'Cradle-snatcher,' the village had called him when the two began living in sin. And some said that she was 'grave-robbing'. The minister at the chapel, encountering Price one day in the street, had dared to ask, 'Why do you not marry that young woman?'

'Marriage,' the doctor had laughed. 'Marriage is an institution that reduces women to slavery.'

When it was known that she was pregnant, there were many who said that a man of 83 could not beget, but there were others who declared that William Price was capable of anything.

'We did our best,' he said, 'but it was not to be. Now we must prepare. You remember our vow, you agreed with me that burying in the earth should not be, that when we die our bodies shall be burned. Let us do the same for our son. Show them that we have the strength of our beliefs. Let us burn Iesu.'

For a while all her conventional upbringing made Gwenllian revolt against the notion. He had converted her to the idea of cremation long ago, but . . . when it came to Iesu . . . no one could be a more subtle persuader than William Price when he tried, and Gwenllian was soon hypnotised by his cajoling, his clever appeals to her loyalty to him while at the same time telling her that she was a free woman, that the choice was hers to be freely made, but making clear also what a great blow to him it would be if she opposed him . . . and he was going to do it anyway. By the morning she had agreed.

Jack Jones and Islwyn Thomas agreed to help, and it was on the Sunday, after dark, that he carried the body wrapped in a sheet to the top of the hill on Caerlan Fields. His two helpers pulled a cart on which rested a wooden box, some coal and a cask of paraffin.

On the hill they made the funeral pyre, and Price applied the light. Folk returning from chapel were making their way along the lane when the flames shot skyward, and the smell of burning flesh wafted down.

A crowd rapidly gathered, and once the cause of the fire was known, fury erupted. Someone ran for the police. Others found a long tree branch and began pushing the box containing the body off the fire.

'Burn the old devil!' and 'Push him into the fire!' were only some of the cries of anger that went up. Price found himself hustled and pushed and several times struck. They rescued the box which had not properly burned through, and Price was rushed away by two constables.

'You have done it properly this time, Doctor Price,' said

Superintendent Matthews in Pontypridd police station, with a note in his voice that might easily have been taken for satisfaction. 'Indeed you have done it. A right proper hole you have got yourself into, isn't it?'

Price, shaken by the mob, but defiant as ever of the world, spoke with seething anger. 'You give me back my son, Matthews; and I will give him a decent civilised burning. Neither you nor those ignorant buffoons will stop me.'

He was released the next day, pending the inquest, and returned to Gwenllian, stalking along the main street of Llantrisant, a glowering, towering figure that no one dared confront, his face like an unfolding map of a tragic country, his boots ringing on the cobbles.

Gwenllian was sitting in the house, surrounded by their four wolf-hounds whose presence made all but a few chosen friends keep a wide berth. He noted that two windows had holes in them.

'Some boys threw stones,' she explained. 'You are tired. I will make you tea.'

He slumped in his big chair. 'I will beat them.' He gripped her hand. 'I will beat all the ignorant world and burn our son. He shall have the funeral he deserves.'

She smiled, for the first time in days, and he reached up to touch the dark lustrous hair, now in tidy ringlets.

'You will beat them,' she told him. 'We will beat them.'

She went into the kitchen, leaving him brooding, carrying with her the image of suppressed volcanic fury on his face, that face which she knew had the art of weaving eyebrows into frowns and in other moods could glow with amusement at the comedy of life. His skin, these days, had a pattern of numerous branching wrinkles.

The inquest was held a few days later, the verdict being death by natural causes. The police immediately made application to the coroner for permission formally to bury the remains, but Price objected and the coroner refused to give the permission. Reluctantly, the police had to return the body, but he was indicted for trial at Cardiff Azzises.

'I must ask your firm promise that you will not burn this body again,' said Superintendent Matthews.

'You will give me back my son and I will do as I wish!'

Matthews had no alternative but to give in, and Price, accompanied by a man with the peculiar name of Y Mochyn Du *(The Black Pig)* collected the body, but, instead of going straight home, they went first to a barn where Price kept a cow which needed feeding. Here they chopped up several buckets of turnips. Four local men had followed them and now stood outside the barn listening to the grisly and sinister sound of chopping!

Imagination ran wild, and more people gathered. When the two emerged from the barn it was to find a menacing crowd. Carrying the body of the child between them, Price and his friend fled for the sanctuary of Tŷ'r Clettwr amid a hail of stones and curses. Not until some of the crowd ventured to enter the barn did they find the true cause of that chopping. It was a farcical incident which could have been serious had the mob turned really violent.

Two days later on Caerlan Fields, Iesu Grist was properly burned with half a ton of coal.

This act of defiance aroused Price's enemies to renewed rage. All over Wales preachers thundered denunciations from their pulpits. One newspaper headline warned against 'the pagan monster in our midst'.

A few nights after the cremation, Price went out for his nightly walk. It had become a custom lately that when he went at night he left the dogs at home for Gwenllian's protection, despite her urging that he could take two of them with him.

He had been gone only 15 minutes when she heard shouting outside, and two large stones came crashing through the window. The dogs howled.

Peering through the smashed panes she saw in the light of a bright moon a mob, mostly composed of women, many with aprons full of stones. Gwenllian quickly grabbed from the wall one of the several pistols that were always available and loaded it. She flung open the door and stood pointing the weapon, the dogs barking furiously round her feet.

'Back!' she shouted. 'I'll shoot the first one past this door!'

The mob paused and milled about, hurling curses, but in the face of that menacing muzzle and the snarling dogs, none of them had the courage to do more. Within ten minutes a small force of police arrived, having been alerted by a Price supporter, of whom there were still several in Llantrisant.

Meanwhile, Price had been spotted by a small crowd as he stalked the main street, having unwisely decided to make his way back through the village instead of circling round by the paths that he knew. Seeing them approaching, he hastened in through the door of the Old Bear Tavern. There were only a few customers inside, and one, fortunately, was Jack Jones. Jack hurriedly pulled the doctor through the back door of the inn, over an adjoining wall and out onto the Common behind Llantrisant, while the crowd poured into the inn.

It was late when Price returned to Tŷ'r Clettwr. 'You outran the hunt, indeed you did,' Gwenllian greeted him, triumph replacing anxiety. 'You old fox. You know the lay of the land better than the pack.'

'Aye, the moon was big and helped me more than it did them, even though it was a sneering moon. Have you not noticed, how the moon sometimes seems to sneer? Even so, I cheated them. We both did, and this time the fox is going to turn round and bite the pack.'

The next few weeks while they waited for the trial was a period fraught with tension. The Superintendent had warned the village that he was there to see that they did not take the law into their own hands. Patients still came to the surgery attached to the house. Many had travelled long distances, and their belief in the doctor's prowess as a healer overcame what opinions they had about cremation, though some expressed their support.

'When this is done,' said Gwenllian one day. 'Let us go away from this place, from these wicked people. We could go to Paris, like you did before when they hounded you. You have said that your soul is eroding here, remember?'

'I remember, but I will not leave. They are not wicked, Gwen; they are just ignorant and stupid. The founder of their religion said that they know not what they do, and He was right. The preachers stand in their pulpits and mouth their words. They should *listen* to the words, not just recite from their old book. I will not leave them, ignorant though they be, and always eager to cast the first stone. My place is here. I cannot touch their souls, if such things' exist, but their bodies need me. All that the other doctors can do is give the potions that just hide the symptoms and cure nothing.'

'You are eighty-four. How long will you go on pushing yourself, working when you do not need to?'

'Until the machine stops, woman; that's until. Do not talk to me of retiring. Life is to be lived. I will wear away, not rust away.'

He touched her cheek. Good health still bloomed in her skin, 'You will wear with me, so that I can hear your laughter, like the rippling of streams over stones in the hills.'

Her gentle smile reflected the gambolling flames from the fire. 'You should have been a poet. You so often talk the language of the poets.'

He moved towards the surgery, necessity triumphing for the moment over other considerations. 'I must prepare my speech for the court.'

While they waited for the Assizes he went about normal business, visiting some patients, often passing through the village, erecting around himself an edifice of truculent indifference. One day a villager dared to stop him. 'Doctor Price, what will happen to our immortal souls if all our bodies are burned instead of being properly buried?'

'If you believe in souls,' Price snapped back, 'do you think that your creator made them of such flimsy materials that they would perish in a mere fire?'

There was no answer to that.

His speech for the defence was complete. He had mobilised and masterminded every argument, taking into account every possible trick that the prosecution could use. Of all his court cases, this was to be the most vital.

In a letter written to Hugh James of Liverpool at this time, he gave vent to his feelings about the constant preaching against him from church and chapel. 'Preachers,' he wrote 'are always on the side of the rich. They are paid to teach that the world of thieves and oppressors, of landlords and coal-owners, is a just world. Their theology is always that of the doctrine that the powers that be are ordained by God. I do not believe in gods or devils, in heavenly creatures, in virgins, in saints, in pious princes, in bishops or landlords, all of whom have been canonised by the crafty priests. Through the ages religion has been used by kings and priests for the enslavement of their fellow creatures.'

The day came. Gwenllian stayed behind to guard the dogs and the cottage, and he travelled alone to Cardiff.

Clad resplendently in a white smock of fine linen with scalloped collar and cuffs and a shawl of royal tartan over his broad shoulders, he made an impressive if bizarre figure.

He refused to swear on the Bible, loftily proclaiming 'I am under the protection of older gods,' but after some argument he condescended to swear on the New Testament.

The official charges were two:

1. For attempting to burn a body instead of burying it.
2. For attempting to burn a body for the purpose of preventing an inquest being held on it.

When his turn to speak came, he prated for two hours, his sails swelled with the gale of a truly Welsh eloquence. The trial had attracted attention far beyond the Principality, and his arguments for cremation were reported by journalists from London, France and the USA. The fame of Dr William Price had never been so widespread.

In his conclusion he said:

'In the ancient world, cremation was common. In fact, it has the respectability of the Book of Genesis in which Abraham is ordered – by God, no less – to prepare the funeral pyre for his son Isaac.

Perhaps the modern opponents of cremation might prefer some higher authority than that given to Abraham (laughter!). There are reports of other cremations throughout the Bible, and in the Greek and Roman civilisations cremation was the normal practice for disposal of the dead.

Opposition to this age-old custom arose when Christianity became dominant. Christians, having discovered the soul and being afraid that it might be of somewhat flammable material, were reluctant to risk it to the fire. For centuries we have been stealing the land from the living, robbing future generations of part of their heritage to make room for decomposing corpses, even though the priests tell us that the souls have gone elsewhere. The first rebellion against this contradictory worship of the empty and vacated body, to the symbol instead of the spirit, came in 1658 when Sir Thomas Browne, a physician of Norwich, member of my own humble profession, published his *Hydriotaphia: Urn Burial*. A few years ago, in 1869, a resolution was put to the Medici International Congress of Florence by professors Coletti and Castiglione, that cremation is now necessary in the name of public health and civilisation. A model of a cremating machine was exhibited at the Vienna Exposition in 1873, and cremation is openly advocated by no less a person than Sir Henry Thompson, Surgeon to our own gracious queen.

'In the *Contemporary Review* of 1874, Sir Thompson wrote that 'Cremation is becoming a necessary sanitary precaution against the propagation of disease among a population daily growing larger in relation to the areas occupied. Cremation would also be a precaution against premature burial, rescue the cost of funerals, and spare the mourners having to stand exposed to the elements. (Price was tactful enough not to mention that Sir Thompson had also made the suggestion that the ashes might also prove a useful fertiliser!)

'The Vikings burned their dead in their long boats, the bodies of Indian princes have long been burned in public. When Byron burned the body of his friend Shelly on a beach in Italy, it could be said that he was merely making a romantic gesture, and that poets are different anyway. But not so in the case of a Captain Hanhan of Dorset who, as recently as 1882 burned the bodies of his wife and mother on his own land. The Home Secretary did not take any action. The time has now come to change old ways for the good of the many.'

He sat down and the jury went out, to return shortly with a verdict of not guilty on both counts.

The summing up of Judge Stephens was brief and to the point.

'Cremation of the dead,' he declared, 'is not illegal provided it is carried out in such a manner as not to constitute a nuisance. I am of the opinion that a person who burns instead of burying a dead body does not commit a criminal act, unless it is done in such a manner as to amount to a public nuisance at common law.'

Thus was cremation made legal in Britain, and the first crematorium opened two years later in Woking as a direct result of that judgement.

Price returned in triumph, and his first act was to commemorate the cremation of Iesu Grist by having struck 3000 oval-shaped bronze medals. Letters by the hundred poured into Tŷ'r Clettwr from all over the world congratulating him, letters from ordinary people and from the famous and distinguished.

An American journalist interviewed him and asked why he and Gwenllian had never married.

'Marriage,' Price explained patiently, 'is of no importance; rather is it the desire to mate which nature endowed in us which makes people complete the union that we call marriage. I have found it unnecessary to enter into any legal marriage because I do not, as an evolved being, require any law or religious ceremony to compel me to love the woman I have chosen as my mate. The artificial thunder of the church and the state on marriage cannot frighten me to live with any woman under compulsion. No law made by God or man can force a man and a woman to love each other, which is quite another thing.'

The widespread publicity and his victory seemed to have stunned the opposition, and Price could not resist rubbing it in. When one of his cows died he ceremonially cremated it on Caerlan Fields.

'Why do you bother tormenting them?' said Gwenllian.

'They tried to tread on my dreams. You, woman, have painted my dreams – in glorious colours.'

But he had not quite finished with the 'tormenting'. Later that year, the *Daily Telegraph* carried the following report:

'At Swansea Assizes yesterday, Mr Justice Grove presiding, Dr Price of Llantrisant brought an action against Police-Superintendent Matthews, Pontypridd, and Sergeant Hoyle, Llantrisant, for alleged wrongful imprisonment, trespass, and detention of the body of his child on the occasion when he attempted to burn it on his property at Caerlan Fields.

'The plaintiff claimed damages amounting to £3,130. The statement of charge, after reciting preliminary particulars, went into the following financial details: For the breaking and entering and wrongful searching and seizure, destruction and injuries on Jan. 15 and 16, 1884, and inclusive of £1.10s the cost paid by the plaintiff for goods, barrel of oil, and of carriage, £30; for the wrongful assault and beating, and taking from the plaintiff's lawful custody the dead body of his child, Iesu Grist, and assaulting and beating the plaintiff, and arresting him and dragging him over Cae yr Lann, Llantrisant, and through the public streets, and imprisoning him, and bringing and falsely charging him before the stipendary magistrate, on Jan. 13, 14, 16, 23 and 30, 1884, and prosecuting him at the assizes in and for the county of Glamorgan, £2,700; for the expenditure and expenses of the plaintiff and his loss of time and professional fees as a medical man, consequent upon the aforesaid charges, and in defending himself therefrom on the aforesaid charges, and in defending himself therefrom on the aforesaid several days of January and February 7 respectively, namely, expenditure and expenses estimated at £50, and loss of time and fees at £60, £100 for the wrongful possession and detention by the defendants of the dead body of the plaintiff's child, Iesu Grist, on Jan. 13, 14, 15 and 16, 1884, £30; for the slander of the plaintiff by the defendants, Jan. 13, 14 and 15 1884, £105; for the expenditure and expenses of the plaintiff and his loss of time before the coroner and professional fees in consequence of the said slander, £25.

Plaintiff gave evidence in support of his own case. He declined at first, on professional grounds, to state who was the mother of the child cremated.

Mr M'Intyre, who appeared for the police, asked him who he believed was the mother?

Dr Price replied that he believed in nothing (laughter).

On being pressed, and the objection being overruled by the judge, Dr Price said that it was likely Gwenllian Llewellyn, his housekeeper, was the mother. He had had many children but had not registered any. He had christened the child himself. Mr M'Intyre having asked whether Dr Price had not expressly contravened the promise he made to the stipendary magistrate about the interment of the child, when it was agreed to deliver it up to him, Dr Price quoted a Welsh adage that it was 'no sin to deceive a deceiver'. (Laughter). His child had been stolen, and an attempt was made to repeat the offence. Did Mr M'Intyre think him such a simpleton as to keep a promise made under such circumstances? The promise he had made to the magisterial bench was without solemnity (Laughter). The stipendary in keeping his child had kept stolen property. He denied that Hoyle had entered his house, when he was at the police station, to protect the housekeeper. The latter would as lief have seen the devil as Hoyle (Laughter). Asked by Mr M'Intyre whether it was true he carried loaded weapons about with him, Dr Price said that he carried more about him than counsel thought.

Mr M'Intyre: 'Then I trust you won't use them on me (Laughter).

The case terminated on Saturday. Damages were awarded to the plaintiff of £3000.

Chapter 9

The Interview

In May, 1888, an enquiring and rather naive reporter from the *Cardiff Times & South Wales Weekly News* set out to interview the famous pioneer of human cremation. Under the headline of *Famous Druid Interviewed*, the account began:

'In the once flourishing but now fast dilapidating town of Llantrisant, there lives at the present day a man whose name is familiar to all, and whose deeds have on more than one occasion been the theme of comment throughout the length and breadth of the United Kingdom. In Glamorganshire, especially, his eccentric actions and his marvellous escapades are frequently dilated upon with manifest enjoyment by some of the older inhabitants whose memories carry them back to the troublous days of the Chartist riots, while there is hardly a cottage in the countryside where the subject of our sketch is not at one time or other the central figure of an exciting tale unwoven on the family hearth. The anecdotes concerning him are innumerable and, although in their passage from mouth to mouth, some of them have been distorted out of all recognition, still most have some foundation in fact and it is questionable whether anyone in his position in life has had a more adventurous career. In some respects he seems to have possessed attributes akin to those of a Salamander, although the mighty engines of the criminal law have several times been put in motion against him, he has never failed to elude their iron grasp, and without having once sought the assistance of a legal advocate. He seems often to have raised his head against the whole community, and to despise all those things that mankind has learned to regard with reverence and respect. In short, it would seem, according to his ideas that whatever is customary is necessarily wrong, and this theory is carried out by him even in the smallest affairs of life.

'According to his peculiar creed, matrimony is to be condemned as an institution which reduces the fair sex to a condition of slavery; the burial of dead bodies is a barbarous practice and should be superseded by cremation; the eating of animal flesh has a tendency to revive in man the worst passions of a brute; vaccination is a method established by law for the purpose of slaughtering infants; the wearing of socks is injurious to health; and lastly, but by no means least, the Christian belief in a Deity and a future spiritual existence is all moonshine.'

The reporter, larding his script with the hyperbole and wordiness that characterised the journalism of the 1880s, at last approaches the actual name of the subject of his interview.

'To most of my readers this hurried sketch will have sufficed to call to their minds the person and peculiarities of the famous Druid, Doctor William Price of Llantrisant, the advocate of cremation, and those who have seen him in the flesh are not likely, I presume, to have soon forgotten the impression his unconventional appearance must have made upon their minds. Doctor Price is a Druid of a very aggressive type, and whether at home in Llantrisant or abroad in the surrounding towns, he is never seen dressed otherwise than in the peculiar garb which he claims to be in all respects similar to that worn by the ancient founders of the Druidic system. Upon his head he wears a huge fox-skin, the tail and legs of which dangle like so many tassels among the snowy locks of his hair, which he allows to grow in plaits of extraordinary length. A white tunic covering a waistcoat made of scarlet cloth and ornamented with brass buttons encircling his body, while his trousers are composed of a green cloth with scarlet stripes, the portion of the cloth above the boots being cut in Van Dyke fashion. 'Time on his head has snowed, yet still 'tis borne aloft.' Despite the fact that he has exceeded by many years the allotted span of life, his body is now as erect and his walk as firm as would put many a younger man to shame. Born with the century, it has been his lot to have been the contemporary of four different occupants of the throne of Britain, to have witnessed the rise and fall of 29 political administrations, and to have taken a by no means insignificant part in those exciting struggles for political and religious liberty which mark the history of the 19th century.'

What Price thought of that reference to his having a part in the struggles for 'religious' liberty we do not know. Obviously, with his irreligious views he would have smiled at such comment. The reporter, however, was in full spate. He had his 'personality profile' and was giving it the full benefit of 19th century journalese.

'Actuated by a desire to see and hear this extraordinary old man, I have for the past few weeks been in the habit of paying him occasional visits at his home in Llantrisant, and during these interviews I succeeded in getting him to relate several reminiscences of his career, which I believed cannot fail to be of interest to the inhabitants of South Wales generally. It was on a cold, bleak morning in March that I found myself for the first time face to face with the famous Druid, of whom I had read and heard so much. What I had heard of him had, of course, led me to expect that his attire would be anything but orthodox, but even the most wild pictures that I had imaginatively drawn of him fell far short of the actual reality which, in Dr Price's own person, opened the door at which I had just knocked. For a time I was speechless, but when I at last screwed up enough courage to address him, and to acquaint him with the object of my visit, his features relaxed, and the ferocious, piercing look gave way to a kind smile, which at once dispelled any fear I had entertained as to my bodily safety. Bless his reverend locks, how that smile of his did cheer me!'

'Ah,' said he, in reply to my query. 'You want a sketch of my life, do you? Well, I must tell you – and here he placed a hand familiarly on my shoulder – 'I must tell you I have made my will and intend to publish it.'

'Indeed,' said I. 'It will prove very interesting, I am sure. Can I have a look at it?'

'It is not ready yet. I have given the necessary directions to have it drawn out, and when it is published, it will show the world what kind of will a character like mine can make. You see, I order that my body shall be burned in a specified place, and I direct that a prescribed quantity of coal shall be used on the occasion; and so, when people read it, they will exclaim "we know very well that Doctor Price's body is to be burned, for he orders it in his will." '

'Then you still believe that cremation is preferable to burying?'

'Certainly. It is already being done in England. The first crematorium was opened there only three years ago, following the burning of my deceased son, as you will know.'

'You direct that your body shall be burned. That, I presume will take place on your death.'

'Death! There is no death, man,' he said. And he gazed fiercely into my face as he spoke. 'That which you call death does not exist except in the imagination.'

'Some people have said that you have stated that you will not die until you are one hundred and twenty.'

The old man was becoming impatient, and a disgusted look spread over his face as he replied almost passionately 'People do not understand me when I speak. They cannot comprehend. They are ignorant. Do you think that I, who have existed upon his earth for ten thousand years, cannot tell what the future has in store for me? Death, indeed. I shall never see death.'

The unfortunate reporter would not have known about schizophrenia, and could not realise that the insidious disease which has afflicted many famous personages throughout history was, at the age of 88, getting its grip on William Price, even though his increasing eccentricity does not seem to have affected his skill as a doctor, nor stopped patients coming to him.

Here, indeed, was a poser, and I almost recoiled with fear from the speaker who advanced this extraordinary theory of immortality with an assurance that appeared to border on blasphemy.

'But, doctor,' I argued. 'If there is no death, why will it be necessary to burn your body? What is it that takes place when the spirit departs from the flesh?'

'Are you a Druid?'

'No.'

'Are you a physiologist?'

'I cannot say that I am.'

'Then you cannot understand these things. But I will show you what I mean. Do you see this child? He indicated a three-year-old playing outside, whose head, like that of the doctor's, was covered by a fox-skin. "That child," continued Doctor Price, "is my son, born since the death of his brother. His name is Iesu Grist, Jesus Christ. I shall in future exist in him. What takes place at death is simply a renewal. I shall exchange this body for that of my offspring. Now do you understand?'

I wished I did, but as I was on the point of putting a further question, a tall, well-built lady came to the door, and suggested with a smile that we 'come in from the cold'. I found myself ushered into a sparsely furnished room and kindly invited to make myself comfortable. This I was nothing loath to do, and having been relieved of my hat, gloves and stick, I drew as near the fire as three or four growling dogs that lay lengthwise on the hearth would allow.

'By the way, Doctor Price,' I remarked, with a view of reopening the conversation, 'I suppose you have heard of Myfyr Morganwg's death? He claimed to be the Archdruid, I believe.'

'Yes, he was a very clever old man, and very well read, but he did not understand, you know. He did not understand.'

'Did you know that Morien claims to be his successor?'

'Does he? Well, Morien knows nothing of Druidism, not he.'

'I presume that you claim to be the Archdruid. Do you intend taking any steps to prove the title?'

'No, I do not. I shall let matters remain as they are. An Archdruid should be able to read and decipher all Druidical letters and hieroglyphics, and Morien knows nothing at all about them.'

'But on what grounds do you claim the title? Was your father a Druid?'

'Yes, my father was baptised in Gallywasted House, in the parish of Machen by Hugh Jones. This was the only place where Druids baptised their sons, and on a gravestone in Machen parish churchyard you will find a very big coat of arms, with an oblong concave dial, which held the water for the ceremony of baptism. There was a clergyman present who, after the ceremony, called my father "My Godson, William Price".'

'But how does this prove your claim to the title of Archdruid?'

'Ah,' said the doctor, chuckling. 'It is funny, it is funny. I can read the arms of the Druids and no one who is not an Archdruid can do that. Hugh Jones, I should tell you, was the owner of Ruperra Estate, which always belonged to the Druids. The owner of Ruperra was supposed to possess a power inherent in him to baptise, and could bequeath the property to whom he pleased. Hugh Jones lives at Machen, and he, in his will, bequeathed Ruperra to my father, and appointed John Morgan of Tredegar, his main executor. John Morgan was a Druid, and Hugh Jones had lent him £40,000 to take possession. My father was thirteen years of age when Hugh Jones died in 1777 but because of a fall which my father had upon his head, he was rendered incompetent to look after his property. I have deposited in the Public Record Office an affidavit of 725 folios in which I trace my right to Ruperra, and have exhibited 120 proofs that I claim the authority that the Primitive Bard had to govern the world.'

'Did you ever seek to recover possession of Ruperra?'

'Yes and proved my claim to it, too, but judgement was given against me. I have traced several important facts on a stone in the hamlet of Llanbedr, and I exhibited the stone itself in the proofs that I speak of. Llanbedr means the Church of Baptism, and no one but a Druid has the right to baptise.'

'Doctor, there is a story I have heard that you exhumed your father's body and cut off his head. Is there any truth in that?'

'Yes. That has been thrown in my face many times as if it was a crime. I conducted a *post mortem* examination of the body in the presence of Doctor Edwards of Caerphilly and Doctor Davies of Bedwas. I was directed to do so by the Court of Chancery.'

'Why was a *post mortem* necessary?'

'We were claiming property in Rudry at the time, and it was necessary for me to prove that my father had been incompetent for many years to manage the estate. The result of the *post mortem* was to show that he had indeed been *non compos mentis*.'

'Who opposed your claim for the recovery of the Rudry property?'

'The defendants were the trustees of the children of Fothergill Hensol, who it was pretended had bought Rudry from my father. Nominally, my eldest brother was the plaintiff, but it was I who really conducted the suit in law and in equity for sixteen years, and spent £4,000 in doing so. My brother was dissatisfied with my management of the case, because, he said, it lasted too long. Well, it was not my fault. Lord Chancellor Cotton, who tried the case, was very much in my favour and gave me the verdict which was upset on appeal. I would certainly have succeeded if my brother had not taken matters into his own hands. Ultimately he became bankrupt, and I never received a penny of the £4,000 I had spent.'

That was the conclusion of my first day's interview with Dr William Price, but a few days later I was allowed to pay another visit to the doctor's house.

I began by saying: 'You have had a very eventful life, and a sketch of your career would be very interesting. I suppose you must have had a very thorough educational training.'

'You may suppose so if you like, but all my schooling cost only £25.'

'Indeed! And how many terms would that sum represent?'

'I paid four shillings per quarter, so you can work out the sum for yourself. I never received a day's schooling before I was ten years of age, and then I used to walk two miles every morning to a little school at Machen kept by a man named Gatwood, on the system of Daniel Lancaster, a peculiar system. It was there that the children of the middle class were taught. Before I had been there two years I had passed through all the cipher books, every one of them, and had learned to speak and write in English. That was no easy task in those days. My father would not talk a word of English with us.'

'How long did you remain in this school?'

'When I was about thirteen, Lancaster offered to appoint me as his assistant at a salary of £20 a year, but I would not accept it. I had learned all that he could teach me and I wanted something better.'

'Had you then a leaning in favour of the medical profession?'

'Yes. I will tell you about it. After leaving school, I was sent to Dr Evan Edwards of Caerphilly. I stayed with him for five years, and when I had been there only a few months, an uncle of mine, Thomas Price of

Somersetshire, came with the intention of sending me back to school. He was furious when I would not go. He had a son, Doctor Charles Price, living in Brighton, and they had got the bulk of my father's property between them. My uncle used to be very kind to me, but on this occasion he was so mad with my refusing Lancaster's offer, that he finally said, "I will not do anything for you again." But I did not care. I did not want his money, and told him so.'

While relating this reminiscence, the doctor chuckled pleasantly, as if thoroughly enjoying the scene it recalled to his mind. Soon afterwards, replying to further questions I put to him, he said:

'I remained five years with Edwards and picked up a knowledge of Latin. I also grounded myself thoroughly in English. It was in 1820 that I first went to London. I stayed there with Daniel Edwards, a brother of Evan Edwards. He was an excellent fellow, a very humane man, but he was not 'flush' any more than myself. We had to help each other as much as possible. He had passed the Royal College of Surgeons but not the Hall, for he had no knowledge of Latin. I had never had a Latin grammar in my hand before I went there, but we studied hard together. However, I passed through the Hall before he was half way through with his Latin. For twelve months afterwards I was attending lectures on anatomy, physiology, surgery and medicine at the Bartholomew and the London Hospitals. I studied hard, I can tell you. I was at it continuously from morning to night.'

'But, doctor, if you say that you were not 'flush' with money, how did you maintain yourself during this period?'

'I had taken care to make a packet before going up, and I used to assist Daniel Edwards at night. I qualified in 1821.'

'What became of you then?'

'There was in London at that time a certain Doctor Armstrong. He was appointed a lecturer on *materia medica* at the school which I had attended in the borough. But he was as ignorant a man as you could meet. He did not know one medicine from another, so he was obliged to put himself under my tuition for four months before he was competent to teach that school which was attended by more than 400 pupils. Oh, I taught him a lot of things – physics, drugs, chemistry – and made him a master of his business. But, mind you, this was a secret. It would not do to let the people know that this great man was under the tuition of Doctor Price. Ha! Ha! But he was. After that I got a lot of persons to ground – sometimes I had as many as 20 or 30 at the same time. I 'grounded' them – they call it coaching these days. At this time I was called upon to attend an old gentleman called John Forbes, who had been to India and had ruined his constitution in a warm climate. I soon found out that I could please him even better than his old medical man could, and when I told him I was going away he became very sad. 'Don't go,' he said, 'for as sure as you go I will die.' So I was compelled to remain with him for a further ten months when he did die. But I prolonged his life I can tell you, by six months or more.'

'Did you stay in London after his death?'

'Not long. I wanted to go to India, but my cousin, Doctor Charles Price, advised me to start a practice in Wales. Acting upon his suggestion, I went to Nantgarw, about seven miles from Cardiff. I was there about seven years when I began to build a house for myself opposite Pentyrch. Mr Blakemoor, the owner of the site, had granted me a lease for 99 years, but he wanted me to do something there against my will, and I refused. "Very well," said he. "I will not give you a lease on the place, and I will not return you a shilling of the money you have spent there." I had spent over £200 and the lodge is there now. I told him I would compel him to do so, and I put him in Chancery and got my money back. My brother, who was in Mr Blakemoor's employ as a clerk at the tin works, was very angry with me for this, and when I went to my brother's house one day – he lived at Pentyrch – he tried to throw me out, but I was the stronger and soon put him on his back and gave him a jolly good licking. He gave notice to leave the works soon afterwards, but as I was a great friend of young William Crawshay, I got a place for him at Cyfartha Works, and he remained there for sixteen years.'

'How many brothers had you?'

'Four brothers and three sisters, but my youngest brother died at the age of three as a result of vaccination.'

'Were they all Druids?'

'No. I am the only Druid of the family.'

'Have you ever been bankrupt,' I asked.

'No, but my creditors tried three times to make me bankrupt, but failed. I remember being arrested once in he Chancery Lane, London, because I had not paid some legal costs. I think it was in 1869 I was arrested on a Saturday afternoon after the bank had closed, so I could not then deposit money as a security to keep me out of gaol. On the Monday I received a note from the Court of Chancery that I was to be declared bankrupt. This was done because my creditors had found that I had withdrawn from the Bank of England the money they intended to pounce upon. I appealed against the notice and deposited £400 with the Commissioner as security until the costs had been taxed, so I got the best of it after all.'

'Were you not once prosecuted for forgery in a will case?'

'No, never, but I know what you refer to. Years ago I was the medical attendant of a man called Thomas Thomas, of Warn, near Nelson. I had been attending him for years. The night before he died he sent for me. As he was much worse, and seeing that he would not live long, I advised him, if he had not made his will, to do so at once as he would be gone by morning. He obeyed and sent for his attorney, who arrived shortly before midnight, but refused point blank to draw up the will, saying it would be better to leave it until the morning. 'What shall I do now, doctor?' the poor man said to me.

'Mr Thomas,' I said, 'would you like me to draw up your will for you? He was delighted, and I there and then wrote under his directions. He was dead before six o'clock in the morning. The will was afterwards disputed and prolonged litigation ensued, but the widow, in whose favour the will was made, was eventually successful.'

'Then there was no criminal charge against you whatsoever in this connection?'

'Certainly not. I cannot conceive how such a rumour circulated.'

'But it is a fact, is it not, that you have several times been criminally prosecuted?'

'Oh, yes. I have been tried on charges of perjury, manslaughter and for cremating my own son, but I have never been convicted.'

The foregoing marked my second visit to the home of Dr Price. On my third visit, Miss Llewelyn was present, and I asked if the lady also believed in cremation.

'Yes, I do,' said she.

'But who is to cremate Doctor Price when he dies?'

'I will,' Miss Llewelyn replied promptly. 'If I had the courage to see my own child cremated, I surely ought not to be afraid to cremate Doctor Price.'

'Were there any peculiar marks on the child's body?'

'Yes, there was on his back a most curious representation of a man on horseback, the horse being seen at full gallop. Even the reins and saddle could be plainly discerned. The mark first appeared when the child was about three weeks old.'

'Are there any marks on the body of this little child whom you have also called Iesu Grist?'

'No, nor are there any on my youngest child – a girl.'

'What name have you given to her?'

'Penelope Elizabeth.'

'Is it true that you did not register the births of any of your three

116

children?'

'Yes, quite true. The doctor does not believe in registering children nor in vaccinating them.'

'But how is it that the authorities do not compel you to register?'

'They have tried, never you fear. They cannot take proceedings against me in respect of the two children now alive because they cannot find out in which parish they were born.'

'But were you not fined for not registering the birth of the child that was cremated?'

'Yes. I was fined two pounds by Judge Gwilym Williams when he was stipendiary at Pontypridd. The prosecution then had to prove that I had given birth to a child but I declined to say whether I was the mother of Iesu Grist that died. One of the witnesses subpoenaed to give evidence against me – an aunt of mine named Ann Davies – was charged with having committed perjury, and she was sent for trial to the Assizes, but at the last moment the case was withdrawn, Mr Spickett stating that there was insufficient evidence against her.'

While I was talking to Miss Gwenllian Llewelyn, the doctor left the room, and on his return he handed to me an oval-shaped medal in bronze which, he said, he had had struck in commemoration of the cremation. 'I have given a larger number of them away,' he said, 'and thousands of them have been sold for threepence each.'

I confess I was sorely puzzled to understand the meaning of the extraordinary inscription which the medal bore, and owing no doubt to my inability to cope with so abstruse a subject, I am afraid that the explanation which the doctor offered served only to make my 'confusion more confounded'. However, I will lay before my readers the explanation as it was given to me.

'The serpent,' he said, 'represents the Cymmerian race and the Cymmerian language, and the only word that is enunciated by the serpent's 'zth' – a hissing sound which is represented by the vowels which surround it. Now, in the goat, the serpent and the letters of his egg, or oval, over his head, I am able to decipher the pedigree of the poet, and it is as follows:

'I will go to sow him who will sow me who will go to sow him,

Who will sow perpetual motion is the Serpent of the Baptism with

The Light of the Brain of the Cymmerian goat.'

'The goat is the scapegoat of the wilderness which governed the world for all eternity, and the serpent circumscribes the world. The verse which you see on the observe side of the medal was composed by me, and a free translation of it would run:

'See Jesus Christ from the fire dragging
In the hand of Victoria, my dear Welshman,
In the presence of the Day of Judgement
He owns the sword,
Of the Prince of Love of the Crown of Wales.'

'Why,' I asked, 'did you call the child Jesus Christ?'
'Because I have the authority for doing so in Gwyll llys fy Nayd (the will of my father). In ancient times the governor or king of the country was always selected by the Druids, and the person whom they chose was called by them Mab Daw (the Son of God). It was for this reason that Cynddelw called Llewelyn, the second Welsh prince of that name, by the title in the following englyn:

'Mab Daw diamhen dy ddawn
A'th ddoniog wyf tinuau
Am dy wir eryr eirau
Am dy wlad wiedig dehau.'

'This prince was baptised by the Druids of Llanfedw.'
'Then do you mean to assert that the child, Jesus Christ, whose body you cremated, would, if he had lived, have reigned over the earth?'
'Certainly, because I have proof positive that I am the son of the Welsh primitive bard, and I am equally certain that the second child of mine, whom I have also called Jesus Christ, will reign on earth and that in him the ancient Druidical system will be restored.'
'What is that which you call Gwyll llys fy Nayd?'
'It is the most splendid thing on earth. During my first stay in Paris, I visited the Louvre, and there came across a precious stone on which was engraved a portrait of the Primitive Bard addressing the moon. In one hand he holds Coelbren y Beirdd, while in the other he has a mundane egg, the image of immortality. Across the body I found inscribed several Greek characters and hieroglyphics, and although the stone has been in existence for two thousand years, I am the only person who has been able to decipher the inscription and I spent twenty years of my life doing so.'
'What did you make it out to be?'
'The characters I told you of represent the Song of the Primitive Bard, the theme of which is Jesus Christ, and it says that his son shall walk

upon the earth again as before. Now, although I have given a challenge, and publicly offered £50 to anyone who would be able to decipher the song, no one except myself has been able to do so. I am the son of the Primitive Bard, and it is this son of mine here, Iesu Grist, that the bard sings about. I therefore call it Gwyll llys fy Nayd. This is a translation of the tablet on the right hand of the bard:

'hast though seen the Strong Lord
The Black Rod of song of the Lords
That sows hell
With my old ocean for the sun to generate me?
He will liberate my country
The Lord in judgement
Enslaved in my temple that gathers whomsoever
You are to serve him who is
'Yes, (who is) 'A' that will go before 'A' I sowed my seed in
The limit of the blockhead god that has no seed in him!
'A' that will go before I shall cease to shed the blood of contending armies
'A' Will go before the glorious foam shall come on my lips
'A' will go before my equivalent power shall come on the wooden wands
Of the poet my soul 'A' will be my equivalent seed
The administrator my will is the letters of books
In the custody of my tongue after I shall see myself liberated
In the sight of those who will look out of my Lord's books
Who will buy the country of heaven to sow my supreme seed.

And here is the translation of the tablet on the left of the bard:

I am a divine and a common Primitive Bard
Who knows every songster
In the cave of the seasons
I will liberate the place where I am confined
In the belly of the stone tower
I will tell your king
And the common people
That a wonderful animal will come
From the shores of the Lord of War
To punish the lies of the bloodhounds of mankind
I will go into his hair, the teeth and eyes of gold in peace

119

And I will visit with vengeance their lies on the bloodhounds of mankind.

All of this may have been a wonderfully lucid explanation of the point I wished to have cleared up with Doctor Price, but somehow or other I did not feel very much enlightened even after I had heard it. However, for policy's sake, as my friend Morien would say, I endeavoured to appear highly gratified, and further, to express great admiration of the doctor's ability, and being anxious to change the subject, I asked my companion whether there was any special meaning to the verse which was printed on the card bearing the child Iesu Grist's portrait?

'Oh, yes,' said he. 'That is the pedigree of Jesus Christ but I will not tell you what it means, for if I did there would be a great commotion among the learned men in all countries. That verse contains a veiled reference to the nose, the eyes, the mouth and other organs of man, but you must not tell this to physiologists.'

What manner of catastrophe would follow the revelation to physiologists of this curious fact I do not know, for, before I had time to persue my enquiries any further, my host brought to the table the latest edition of the British Medical Directory, and called my attention to the entry therein relating to himself. It was as follows:

William Price VSLM Llantrisant, Glamorgansh MRCS Eng. LSA 1821 (St Barthol and London) Author of *The Pedigree of Jesus Christ*. Discoverer of Gavval, Lann, Barren Myrrdhdhiu Wyllt, Tyurn, Wislann, Lyurr, Aneurin, Gwawtrudb, Avenoudh, Privv, Varrdb, Nuadh y Btunn, Swann Gwialenn, Laun ab Bayl ap Peyl, Sarrph Yous Pruttain, A ycb Choyal brenn Privv Varrydd Dusc Cymmru a 'Gwyll-llis ya Nayd' decipherer of 'Gwyll-llia Yayd'.

'This,' explained the doctor, 'was written by me, and, as you can see, it describes not only my qualifications as a medical man, but also my Druidical discoveries. I am surprised, though, that the printers succeeded in spelling the Welsh words so correctly.'

'Oh, they are Welsh words, then?' I exclaimed, in a tone which must have betrayed no little surprise, for, though I pride myself on a knowledge of the vernacular, I failed to see the slightest resemblance to it in the foregoing extract.

'Welsh? Of course they are. But my orthography is very different to that in general use. I write as the old bards used to write. And that is the proper way to do it after all. People do not know how to write Welsh these days.'

'Are you a veterinary surgeon, doctor?' I see those letters after your name. What do they signify?'

'That is a secret, but I do not mind telling you. You must read those letters in Welsh. VSLM means Fi si Li Mer. Do you see?'

'Indeed I do not. What is Fi si Li mer?'

'It means 'I am the flood of the ocean.' The Primitive Bard, you know, represented himself as the source of the ocean. Perhaps you have noticed that one of the emblems of Freemasonry is a board with water flowing out of its centre. That represents the Primitive Bard. It is said that it was Newton who discovered that the moon influences the movements of the sea, but that was well known to the Druids thousands of years before he was born.'

The next question which I put to the doctor was whether he believed in the existence of a Deity. His reply was a curious one.

'I believe in nothing, except what is absolutely in existence. I use the Bible as it ought to be used. It is clear to me that Abraham was a cannibal, and it was with a view to destroying that trait in the nature of his descendants, and to raise tame animals, that the first pyramid in Egypt was built.'

'But you do not eat animal food, do you?'

'No, I am a vegetarian and have been for forty years. I contend that human beings ought not to eat animal food, and the Cymmerian teachers and the bards forbade it. The man who eats animal foods descends to the level of the brute, and will in time acquire the habit and passions of the brute.'

'Do you wear stockings, doctor?'

'No. I have not done so for many years because I feel that stockings prevent the proper exhalation of the feet which, in consequence are kept damp, and the person who wears them is more liable to catch cold. My feet are always dry and warm.'

'Have you any particular reason for wearing that fox fur on your head in place of an orthodox hat?'

'Oh, dear me, yes. The fox is represented as one of the highest beings in the hieroglyphics of ancient Egypt. The Primitive Bard and the Druids always wore fox fur head coverings.'

'Do you ever visit the Rocking Stone now?'

'Yes, I go there occasionally.'

'What is it that you do when you go to the Stone? Do you worship something?'

'Worship? I worship nothing. I have not seen anything or anybody greater than myself to worship. All I do when I get there is to chant a song of the Primitive Bard to the moon. Talking of the Stone – there would have been a fine institution there if I had had my way. I once tried to get a school and a tower erected there, but the attempt fell through for want of support.'

'When was it that you endeavoured to bring this about?'

'It must be fully fifty years ago. But here, read this. It is a circular I had printed at the time.'

The document handed to me by the doctor bore the imprint 'W. Bird, Cardiff', and was dated March 7, 1838. Believing it will prove of interest to my readers, I append a copy herewith:

Y MAEN CHWYF

My Lords, Ladies and Gentlemen:

I beg to call your attention, and all those who may feel interested in the preservation of the Ancient Institutions and Antiquities of Britain, and especially in this PRIMITIVE TEMPLE 'Y MAEN CHWYF'. This Druidic temple is situated on the left bank of the Taff, near Pont-y-Ty Perydd, on the verge of the precipice, a little north-east of the nearby Works.

In the immediate vicinity of this temple, the graves of the aborigines occupy a space of about 40,000 square yards.

While the population of this neighbourhood continued to follow agriculture, Y Maen Chwyf was in no danger of being injured, as the hereditary veneration which descended from father to son, through successive generations, was sufficient to shield it from rude hands. But it is not so now.

The legions of artificers, manufacturers and strangers that advance on this place from all directions, have no idea of reverence for this beautiful temple.

Hence it is that some few years ago an attempt was made to destroy it. Mr Thomas of Yuydyngharad heard of it just in time to save it from ruin.

From this brief history, it appears that it requires no great genius to foretell the fate that awaits this most ancient monument.

Under this impression, it was suggested to 'Cymdeithas y Maen Chwyf' that a tower of 100 feet high be built by public subscription near Y Maen Chwyf; the space within the tower to be divided into 8 apartments for a museum and surrounded with a camera obscura. This tower will command a horizon of about ten miles radius. And that a spacious house, some distance from Y Maen Chwyf be built for the bard

122

of the society to reside in and to take care of the temple.

This proposition has been unanimously seconded by the society and the whole neighbourhood, as will be seen by the subscribers' names in the order given.

The estimated cost of these erections is £1000. The revenue of the Tower will be about £100 per annum. With the greater part of this sum the society will establish a Free School to be kept by the Board of the Society for educating the children of the poor. The remainder will go to defray the expenses of the Institution. In this way Y Maen Chwyf will not only be preserved but will continue to operate as a mighty engine of civilisation, the nucleus of a museum, the parent of the Tower that is designed to protect it, and to dispense the blessings of education to the industrious classes of the community.

Y Maen Chwyf will represent the seed: the Tower, the tree, and the inimitable landscape of the camera obscura, the fruit of knowledge. A question has been asked, will the brinker landlords – viz.: Lord Dynevor, B. Hull Esq. M.P., J. Bennett Esq., Mrs Morgan, the Honourable R.H. Clive, and the Marquess of Bute, permit the Bards to protect and preserve their temple? Our answer has been and is, we have no doubt they will not only charter our prescriptive right to protect the Druid's temple, but express their sense of approbation by directing their names to be added to the list of subscribers for its preservation.

'One common cause makes millions of one breast,
Slaves of the East, or Zealots of the West;
On Andrs' or on Athos' peaks unfurled
The self-same standard streams o'er either world.'

As some may question the applicability of the world temple at the present day to designate an immense and poised fragment of rock, on an elevated plain, with no other covering than that of the sky, I beg leave almost humbly to submit that it is infinitely more deserving of that term than the Temple of Jupiter Ammon in Thebes. As none will dispute, I think, Thomson's description of this temple, not made of hands, I shall give it here to illustrate this opinion:

'Nature attend! In every living soul,
Beneath the spacious temple of the sky,
In adoration join; and ardent raise
One general song.'

In this and in similar temples, the music, the language and institutions of the Britons made their first impressions on the infant and savage brain.

In this and similar temples civilisation was born, nursed and educated, under the tuition of men of genius.

In this and similar temples, the uncivilised Britons first acknowledged the dominion of superior intelligence.

In this temple the bards received their degrees of proficiency in the arts and sciences from age to age, from time immemorial to this present day.

In this and in similar temples, opinion, the Queen of the Universe, was created to govern the rulers of the earth.

As Y Maen Chwyf *is the* temple where civilisation was born, let the modern Britons of all grades of opinion second the motion of the Cymreigyddion Society of Newbridge, with the means to protect and preserve to the latest posterity this sublime temple of antiquity, where, perhaps, the remains of the genius of 'Serdi Hudol' and 'Gadlys' lie buried unknown.

Let the respect and reverence we owe to the unknown benefactors of mankind inspire us with gratitude to preserve and protect Y Maen Chwyf as a monument of their superior intelligence.

Let Y Maen Chwyf be the banner of civilisation, around which millions yet unborn shall assemble to learn the music, the language and institutions of the Britons.

Here stands the temple wide as the horizon is, high as heaven is, infinite as time is where all shades of opinion shall never blush to assemble in the face of day and night and in the eye of light.

"T'is come, the glorious morn! The second birth,
of heaven on earth. Awakening nature hears,
The new creating word and starts to life,
In every heightened form, from pain and death
For ever free.

Subscriptions will be received for the protection and preservation of Y Maen Chwyf by the treasurer, Philip Thomas Esq., Ynysyngharad, Newbridge, by the West of England and South Wales District Bank, and by the Merthyr Bank, and gratefully acknowledged by the secretary, William Price, Surgeon, Porthyglo, near Newbridge.

'How was it, doctor,' I asked, 'that the project fell through?'

'Well, the Chartist movement started about this time and interfered with it.'

'What became of the subscriptions?'

'They were never collected.'

'Who was Mr Philip Thomas who acted as secretary?'

'He was manager of the Pontypridd Chain Works, and it is in commemoration of his good work that the famous "Stranger, Halt!" stone was put on Pontypridd Common. The stone was originally placed by Mr Frank Crayshaw over Mr Thomas' grave in Glyn Taff churchyard as a token of respect; but Mr Thomas' son-in-law, a Mr Irving, took offence because it was such an ugly thing, and had it removed. Mr Crayshaw then, at my request, gave the stone to me and I had it put up on the Common where it is now.'

'Did you not taken an active part in the coal strike of 1871?'

'I wrote a great deal at the time and spoke at meetings in favour of the men, but a person who called himself 'Belted Will' wrote against the strike in the papers, and tried to prejudice the men against me. But I gave him quietus at last.'

'Indeed, in what manner?'

'By composing and publishing this verse:

To the Sane and Peaceful Welsh Colliers
of the Aberdare and Rhondda Valleys, lately on
strike against their Pharaohs.

'Strange that such difference should be
'Tween wheedle you and wheedle me'
And Stranger Bill, that 'Belted Will'
With O--M--Hand and Quill!
Should analyse his 'B C' Bubble!
To save the Doctor's Ink and Trouble
Save me? No! You Twaddling Donkey
Balaam's Ass is not so empty!'

'He made no attempt to reply to that.'

This brought to an end my interview with this remarkable man, and, as I wended my way home, meditating on all I had seen and heard, that famous quotation from Hamlet came to my mind with greater force than it ever did before.

'There are more things in heaven and earth, Horatio,
Than are dreamed of in our philosophy.'

Chapter 10

The Cleansing Fire

1892. It was the year that Keir Hardie was elected as the first Labour MP. William Gladstone had become Prime Minister. Bernard Shaw had written *Mrs Warran's Profession* and had it banned by the Lord Chamberlain. Oscar Wilde's *Lady Windermere's Fan* was having its first performance in London. Tchaikovsky's *Nutcracker Suite* was being played for the first time in St Petersburg, and in Paris the Belle Epoque was in full swing with Toulouse-Lautrec sitting in his corner sketching the girls of the Moulin Rouge.

It was also the year when William Price was thrown out of his carriage when his horse slipped on an icy road.

They carried him home and laid him on the couch in the front room at Ty'r Clettwr. 'You have laid me down at last,' he said. 'It is unlikely that at ninety two I shall rise again.'

It was, for him, an unusually pessimistic comment, and on this occasion he did rise again, but it took all his power and determination to win this battle, but win it he did, and after a few weeks was back on his feet, but the battle had taken its toll; the machine was packing up and he did not recover his usual bounce and energy. He gave up visiting patients. They had to come to him now, and come they still did, despite his age and increasing eccentricity; his fame as a healer was so well established that the sick came from far and wide to consult him.

Visitors to Llantrisant always took the opportunity to stroll casually past Ty'r Clettwr in the hope of catching a glimpse of the famous doctor in his fox-skin head covering. When he did go out, he never failed to attract attention.

Early in January, 1893, he suddenly became very weak, and was forced to take to his bed. A doctor who lived nearby, was called in and told Gwenllian that the end was obviously near.

Price's brain was still alert and he was not in pain. On the 22nd, he awoke shortly before nine o'clock in the morning and complained of thirst. Iarlles, Megan's daughter, who had come from Cardiff to help attend to him, asked what would he like. 'Give me champagne,' he demanded, loudly and clearly. She gave him a glass, and shortly after drinking it he died.

William Price had never had any fear of death. He remained to the end convinced that life was merely a blind struggle for survival, driven by nature's remorseless need for each generation to be succeeded by another. He derided the wish-fulfilment myths of religion, he did not call for a priest, he repented of no sins and regretted nothing. His final request on earth was typical – a glass of champagne!

He had made careful and detailed arrangements some months before as to his cremation. Although the first official crematorium in Britain, at Woking, had been functioning for some years as a direct result of his trial at Cardiff Assizes, there had still not yet been a cremation in Wales. This was to be the first under the new laws.

His will directed that no mourning should be worn and that the burning should take place where he directed, the exact spot having been delineated by a 60-foot high pole which he had placed on the Caerlan Fields, topped by a crescent shape representing a new moon.

There were to be no prayers said over him. His body was to be clothed as at the moment of death and the funeral pyre to consist of adequate timber with two tons of coal. The ashes to be scattered to the winds to help 'grass to grow and flowers bloom'. Gwenllian and her two children to be executors.

The cremation was arranged for January 31, and several hundred tickets were issued to those who applied. The tickets gave the time as noon, but on the previous day, for some unknown reason, the time was advanced to 7 am. Spectators began arriving in Llantrisant as early as 3 am, determined not to miss the show.

An estimated 20,000 people crowded into the village that morning. It was the biggest thing ever to hit Llantrisant and the pubs ran out of beer! Many villagers, not slow to scent a profit, hurriedly made up packs of sandwiches for sale.

In the consulting room at Ty'r Clettwr, the clay that had been William Price lay in the iron casket that he had long had prepared. It was encircled by strong bands of iron and covered with white muslin. Price had designed the casket himself and had it made by the local blacksmith, Thomas Jones Talbot.

At 7 a.m. the undertaker, Ebenezer Davies, arrived accompanied by 12 strong men as pall bearers. They lifted the casket onto a bier, and the procession began its journey to the Caerlan Fields. Immediately behind walked the two young children, the boy in a fox-skin head covering similar to the one his father had worn for so many years. A suit of green cloth with red braid was scalloped at the knees. The girl was in traditional Welsh pais a betgwn with a red shawl. Iarlles followed, also in traditional costume. Behind came Gwenllian in a black cloak.

That those responsible for organising the ceremony at the Caerlan had decided to have a Christian service, would surely have aroused the derision of the old heretic, but an orthodox service was read in Welsh. It was spoken by the Rev. Daniel Fisher, a local curate who, defying his church, used for the first time in Wales the words 'consigned to the fire' instead of the usual 'consigned to the earth'.

At 8.15 am Dr Anderson, who had attended Price at the end, applied a lighted torch to the pyre which had previously had several gallons of paraffin poured over it. A breeze fanned the flames in front of the thousands who had gathered to watch. The casket was soon red hot, with tongues of flame licking through the holes that had been bored in the sides.

At 4 p.m., using long iron hooks, several men drew the casket from the smouldering pyre. When it had cooled, the ashes were scraped out and scattered to the wind.

Back in Llantrisant, enterprising people were busy selling photographs and other souvenirs of the village's famous citizen.

No one had dared to publish scurrilous material about William Price while he lived, but after the cremation it was a different matter, and one of the choicest examples is this folk song by Meic Stephens:

'There once was a man called Dr Price
Who lived on lettuce, nuts and rice
His idols were the Moon and Sun
And he walked the hills with nothing on.

Chorus:

Singing I don't care a bugger (repeat three times)
What anybody thinks of me.

The Doctor had a theory
That love and medicine are free,
For many years all over Wales
He used to practise on females.

The randy Doctor in his day
Put lots of girls in the family way
His little bastards could be seen
From Pontypool to Pontyclun.

The Nonconformists didn't like
The practices of Doctor Price
They said he wasn't nice to know,
He had an enormous libido.

So at the age of eighty-eight
The Doctor had to choose a mate,
He met a girl called Gwenllian
And became the father of her son.

A doting dad was Doctor Price,
He called the baby Jesus Christ.
He wrapped it in a flannel shawl,
The bonniest bastard of them all.

But one year later, sad to say
The Doctor's baby passed away,
So after chapel one dark night,
He set the little corpse alight.

The Doctor thought it was a joke
To watch the kid go up in smoke
He took the ashes with a grin
And kept them in a biscuit tin.

But when the local deacons saw
That Doctor Price had broke the law
They shouted at him 'Ach y fi'
And put him under lock and key.

The Doctor told the Magistrate
He didn't care about his fate –
'It was the most hygienic way
I'll be a famous man one day.'

The morning that the Doctor died
His children stood at his bedside
He drank a bottle of champagne
And started singing once again.

He told his children in his Will
To burn him on Llantrisant Hill
They built a crematorium
And the Doctor went to Kingdom Come.

It's thanks to Dr William Price
That modern corpses have the choice
To linger in the mouldering clay
Or go up the chimney straight away.

This immortal verse, the writer of which had got the dating wrong anyway, was discovered by Mr P. Meazey of Penarth, and published in 1966 by the Triskel Press under the title of *Broadsides*.

The memory of William Price was eventually and officially perpetuated in 1947 when a party of delegates to the first Cremation Conference held in Wales, made their way through the narrow streets of Llantrisant to witness the unveiling of a plaque presented by the Cremation Society of Great Britain.

Present to do the unveiling, on the wall of the Zoar Chapel, was Miss Penelope Price, that same daughter who, 54 years before, had walked as a child behind the casket of her father.

The proceedings opened with the remarks of Councillor Ivor Jacob, the town's representative on the Rural District Council: 'You are here today to pay tribute to the memory of an illustrious resident of this old town, and I am pleased and happy to have with us Miss Penelope Price, the daughter of that man. We residents share with her the joy she is experiencing today. The plaque which she will shortly unveil is a fitting tribute to a great man, and I accept it on behalf of the Llantrisant Town Trust. Now I call upon Mr Arthur Pearson, MP, to conduct the proceedings on behalf of the Cremation Society and the Federation of British Cremation Authorities.'

Mr Pearson said: 'It must be a thrill for the organisers to have such a response as is evidenced by the attendance of the delegates of the Cremation Conference who have come from far and near, the Chairman and members of neighbouring Authorities and the Lord Mayor of Cardiff.

'It is fitting that we in this fine old county should commemorate those of her sons who, against ignorance and opposition, faced their trial with great courage, and succeeded in the days of small beginnings to make the event the most historic in this old town of Llantrisant. Dr Price, himself, established in the High Courts the right to cremation and now in these days an ever-widening circle of our countrymen are appreciating the pioneering work of Dr Price in this field. We pay tribute to his memory and we are proud to think that a member of his family is here to perform the ceremony of unveiling this plaque. As your Parliamentary member, I feel it a great honour to ask Miss Price on behalf of the Cremation Society and the Federation of British Cremation Authorities, and also on behalf of the townspeople of Llantrisant and of this County, to unveil this plaque in the memory of her father, Doctor Price.'

Miss Price said, 'I am proud and happy to unveil this plaque in memory of my father and hope it will be preserved for all time. She then pulled the cord which parted the curtain to reveal the bronze tablet with its inscription:

'This Tablet was erected by the Cremation Society and the Federation of British Cremation Authorities to commemorate the act of Dr William Price who cremated the body of his infant son on Caerlan· Fields, Llantrisant. For this act, he was indicated at the Glamorganshire Winter Assizes on the 12th February, 1884, where he was acquitted by Mr Justice Stephens, who adjudged that cremation was a legal act. Thus was legal sanction given to the practice of cremation.'

Miss Price was presented with a silver salver as a memento of the occasion and the proceedings ended with everyone joining in the hymn 'Guide me O thou Great Jehovah' to the appealing strain of 'Aberystwyth' and, finally, that yearning, triumphant 'Hen Wlad Fy Nhadau'.

In the last years of William Price there were many signs of the tragic degeneration of a once fine brain, as he succumbed at last to the evil of schizophrenia. In modern times, it is said that the symptoms freely express themselves in a manner the essence of which is that the meaning of a statement is never quite contained within that statement, but lies somewhere beyond it, and, when searched for, continually retreats behind further elusive statements. It was to that condition that the reporter who interviewed the doctor in the previous chapter found himself exposed.

The type of schizophrenia from which Price suffered is known as Paraphrenia. His weird method of dressing, his sometimes aggressive nature, and confusion of thought as revealed in the near-gibberish of some of his poems, leave no doubt about the medical diagnosis.

Dr John Cule, in a paper read to a meeting of the History of Medicine Section of the Royal Society of Medicine on March 6, 1963, said:

'Litigation is frequently a hobby of a schizophrenic. In it he can find a means of expressing his paranoia, apparently acceptable to society. And in the civil courts Dr Price was able to find this expression which he believed added to his stature. His position as a general practitioner in a small Welsh village gave him a relative invulnerability to criticism. The doctor was regarded with awe and respect and it was not easy to question his views, even if they were somewhat bizarre. For even then doctors did not take kindly to criticism! In this connection it is interesting to note that Laubscher in Cape Province has found that many witch doctors are schizophrenic, their symptoms being masked by the cultural roles they assume.'

In 1982 a further memento of William Price appeared in Llantrisant. This was the modern sculpture of the doctor by artist Peter Nicholas, created through the support of the Welsh Arts Council and the Taff Ely Borough Council. This now stands in the town's Bull Ring. An impressive, modernistic figure with, in the words of the sculptor 'a plain cloak tightly encasing the figure, giving stature to the man and at the same time suggesting an imminent metamorphosis.'

Thus has the wizard of Llantrisant been at last honoured by his own community.

ADDENDUM

Although Price's victory at the Cardiff Assizes had given legal sanction to human cremation, the practice was slow to take off in Wales, and the Cremation Society still has only 12 crematoria in the Principality. However, in 1996 there was founded the Crematoria Investment Company Ltd, a newcomer to the field which aims to bring high standards of design and technology to crematoria. An innovation by this company was the hiring of a stand at the 1996 National Eisteddfod in Llandeilo. With a glossy brochure printed in Welsh, the aim was to imprint the idea of cremation on the Welsh consciousness, and to publicise the new crematorium planned at Llanelli. There is already one at Aberystwyth, the gardens of which have been set out in co-operation with the Dyfed Wildlife Trust.

Price would be pleased to know that his favoured 'way out' is gaining popularity in his own country.

SOURCES

A Welsh Heretic by Islwyn ap Nicholas (Ffynnon Press, 1941).

Dr William Price (1800-1893) by Dr John Cule, a thesis for the University of Cambridge, 1960.

The Colliers' Strike in South Wales by A. Dalziel, 1872.

Dr William Price and Old Llantrisant (Pub. Taff-Ely Borough Council, 1982).

The National Library of Wales.

Mid-Glamorgan Libraries.

South Wales Miners' Library.

The Cremation Society of Great Britain.

The London Hospital Gazette.

'Broadsides' by P. Meazey (Triskel Press, 1966).

Royal Society of Medicine.

Royal College of Surgeons of England.

Mr Brian Davies, Curator Pontypridd Historical and Cultural Centre.

Letters of Dr Price and Vanessa Lawrence.

Daily Telegraph, 1884.

Index